"Jan Johnson's *Invitation to the Jesus Life* is a much-needed response to Dallas Willard's startling charge in *The Divine Conspiracy* that a curriculum of Christlikeness does not exist. It is a carefully crafted 'soul school' for all who are weary with the wrong question — WWJD? — and long to learn how to love as many moments of their lives as possible with him as students of kingdom living."

— GARY W. MOON, MDiv, PhD, vice president and
professor, Renovare Institute

"With simplicity and depth of insight Jan Johnson carves a path of walking with Jesus that feels like a cool glass of water among trivial alternatives. *Invitation to the Jesus Life* is a welcomed guide to following Jesus that is biblical, practical, and most of all *possible*."

— KEITH J. MATTHEWS, DMin, professor of spiritual formation and
contemporary culture, Azusa Pacific University's School of Theology

D0367548

1992

INVITATION TO THE

JESUS LIFE

EXPERIMENTS IN CHRISTLIKENESS

JAN JOHNSON

NAVPRESS

A NavPress resource published in alliance
with Tyndale House Publishers, Inc.

NavPress is the publishing ministry of The Navigators, an international Christian organization and leader in personal spiritual development. NavPress is committed to helping people grow spiritually and enjoy lives of meaning and hope through personal and group resources that are biblically rooted, culturally relevant, and highly practical.

For more information, visit www.NavPress.com.

Invitation to the Jesus Life: Experiments in Christlikeness

Copyright © 2008 by Jan Johnson. All rights reserved.

A NavPress resource published in alliance with Tyndale House Publishers, Inc.

NAVPRESS and the NAVPRESS logo are registered trademarks of NavPress, The Navigators, Colorado Springs, CO. *TYNDALE* is a registered trademark of Tyndale House Publishers, Inc. Absence of ° in connection with marks of NavPress or other parties does not indicate an absence of registration of those marks.

Cover design by studiogearbox.com
Cover photo by Nicholas Belton/i-stock

Scripture quotations marked NIV are taken from the Holy Bible, *New International Version,* *NIV.* Copyright © 1973, 1978, 1984 by Biblica, Inc.° Used by permission. All rights reserved worldwide. Scripture quotations marked NASB are taken from the New American Standard Bible,° copyright © 1960, 1962, 1963, 1968, 1971, 1972, 1973, 1975, 1977, 1995 by The Lockman Foundation. Used by permission. Scripture quotations marked MSG are taken from *THE MESSAGE* by Eugene H. Peterson, copyright © 1993, 1994, 1995, 1996, 2000, 2001, 2002, 2005. Used by permission of NavPress Publishing Group. All rights reserved. Scripture quotations marked NRSV are taken from the New Revised Standard Version Bible, copyright © 1989, Division of Christian Education of the National Council of the Churches of Christ in the United States of America. Used by permission. All rights reserved. Scripture quotations marked CEV are taken from the Contemporary English Version, copyright © 1991, 1992, 1995 by American Bible Society. Used by permission. Scripture quotations marked KJV are taken from the *Holy Bible*, King James Version.

Some of the anecdotal illustrations in this book are true to life and are included with the permission of the persons involved. All other illustrations are composites of real situations, and any resemblance to people living or dead is coincidental.

Library of Congress Cataloging-in-Publication Data

Johnson, Jan, 1947-
    Invitation to the Jesus life : experiments in Christlikeness / Jan Johnson.
        p. cm.
    Includes bibliographical references (p.   ) and index.
    ISBN 978-1-60006-146-2
    1. Jesus Christ—Example. 2. Spirituality. I. Title.
    BT304.2.J64 2008
    232.9'04--dc22
                                    2008011692

Printed in the United States of America

21   20   19   18   17   16   15
11   10   9   8   7   6   5

NAVPRESS BOOKS BY JAN JOHNSON

Enjoying the Presence of God
When the Soul Listens
Savoring God's Word
Renovation of the Heart in Daily Practice

OTHER BOOKS BY JAN JOHNSON

When Food Is Your Best Friend (and Worst Enemy)
Surrendering Hunger
Habakkuk: Staying Sane in a Crazy World
Healing Hurts That Sabotage the Soul
Living a Purpose-Full Life
The Autobiography of Jeanne Guyon (ed.)
Growing Compassionate Kids
Dallas Willard's Study Guide to The Divine Conspiracy
Spiritual Disciplines Bible Studies

To the "council":
Jane,
Keith,
Becky,
Bill,
and Dallas

Contents

Foreword

Confidence in Jesus himself, an awareness that he truly is the Master of the Universe and knows with absolute clarity what is real, good, and right, draws us to him as Savior, Lord, and Teacher, all in One. That is whole-life faith in Christ. It naturally leads us into longing to do what he says, and, so far as possible, to be what he is, by receiving his life in us. For many professing Christians, however, that longing leads only to a life of frustration and disappointment, for they lack adequate practical teaching on how to go about it. Many simply give up and wait for heaven after death, developing a theology of sin and salvation to meet the failures they perceive as a necessity. Others struggle onward, but with small progress judged in terms of the clear benchmarks of the New Testament — say, 1 Corinthians 13. Still others turn aside from faith in Christ, convinced that it "just doesn't work."

The familiar question "What would Jesus do?" is by now notorious for failing to lead people into routine, easy obedience to Christ. Most of those who could sincerely ask the question already have a pretty good idea of what he would do in given circumstances, though there are cases of real doubt. Often they clearly *know* the answer to this question but have no idea of how to put it into practice or of how to live a life of regular practice. Indeed, it would be instructive to pay attention to what is really on the mind of one who asks that question; but it is, in any case, certain that the question "What would Jesus do?" will be of little benefit to serious seekers until they link it to the deeper question "*How* would Jesus do it?" Answers to the former question will prove baffling, and very likely disastrous, if put into action without detailed answers to the latter.

Finding out *how* Jesus would do what Jesus would do is the gift that comes to us as we go to what Jan Johnson calls "soul school" with Jesus. There we learn though patient practice with him the inner texture of the experiences involved in becoming and in being one who reliably does what Jesus said and did in the manner he did it. The manner is, of course, everything, and it alone, when right, can save us from life-destroying legalism and pharisaism, by opening the founts of intelligent grace in our souls and bodies. In soul school with Jesus we learn what actually goes on in the person who is receiving the grace of God as he or she does the things Jesus told his followers to do. And we learn specific ways of becoming one who does that. It isn't impossible, and, indeed, it isn't even particularly hard, except for those who try to do it without integrating Christ the Savior and Teacher into the occasions and moments of action. For them it *is* impossible. But his yoke is easy and his burden is light, and under them we find rest through goodness and strength. So he invites us to come to him and learn of him.

An unsuspecting reader of the New Testament might think that this is precisely what the Christian life is all about. You might get the same idea from looking at those who have actually found their way into effective Christlikeness. The witness is clear to those who will consider it. But the "how" of it all is currently obscured. Thus, what we routinely do in church is not, to say the least, emphatically focused on the transformation of attendees into Christlikeness, from the inside out. While we have, for the most part, just drifted into our distracted condition, moving out of it and making such transformation our overriding aim is a choice we can make. But we need specific, practical instruction as to exactly what we are choosing.

Jan Johnson is a careful student of the biblical texts who knows how to lead us into the experiences that make the Christ-life real in the concrete circumstances where we live. What is it like in our real life, for example, to attend to people as Jesus did, to live without fear, to serve as he served, to die to self, and so forth? She has a deep knowledge of Scripture, on the one hand, and of spiritual life in Christ, on the other. The first application of this knowledge is always to me, the individual, drawn to Christ and intent on becoming like him as his student in kingdom living. But of course this student status is necessarily a life in community with others, some of whom may have other things on their minds or may care nothing at all for Christ, regardless of what they profess. As I learn to open my moments and hours to him, he intermingles his life with mine in all contexts and shows me how to orient every aspect of my being toward him, no matter what is going on around me.

But we are also called by him to lead others into discipleship and then to teach them how to live that same kind of life: "Teach them to do everything I have told you," he said (Matthew 28:20, CEV). Really! It seems to me that, today, very few people know how to do that, and perhaps fewer still see that as *the* task of God's people in our world. You can judge for yourself concerning this matter by observing what our various Christian gatherings and churches actually do or try to do. If in our Christian group, whatever that may be, we were to decide to actually do what the Great Commission says (Matthew 28:18-20), we would need to know how to go about it. We would have to deal with the fine texture of the inner life, the spiritual, psychological, and social dynamics that actually move us in what we do and do not do. How, then, could we set up our Christian activities actually to accomplish what the Great Commission calls for?

Jan Johnson gives a substantial answer to this question, and one that I think is without parallel among contemporary writers. Many older writers, such as Jeremy Taylor and Richard Baxter, to name only two of the most outstanding, also provided answers to this question, in a day when it was assumed that Christian ministers would do so; but they are almost totally inaccessible to the contemporary reader. Jan Johnson has written a *Holy Living* (by seventeenth-century author Jeremy Taylor) for our time, and anyone who understands and does what she says will find such living, as promised, to be easy and light, full of goodness, grace, and strength — regardless of circumstances.

—*Dallas Willard*

1 Soul School: Will I Ever Change?

"What would Jesus do?" is a good question. As a teen I read that phrase over and over in Charles Sheldon's book *In His Steps*. I loved this story of how people changed to become like Jesus, but it seemed like a fairy tale. Many lovely people at my church went the extra mile, forgave terrible people, and died to self, but I was mostly concerned with having a blemish-free complexion and getting A's (in that order). As I grew older, I didn't change much. I wanted to have a meaningful job, be a good wife and mom, have a nice house, and live a life free of major tragedies. When I had time, I'd help people.

To even think about the question "What would Jesus do?" seemed futile because the gap between the person I wanted to be (because I truly admired Jesus) and my everyday self seemed too wide to manage. I *knew* what Jesus would do — compassionate and courageous actions — but I struggled just to be nice to people. I felt almost as inadequate as my son, Jeff, did when as a teen he told me it was easy to know what Jesus would do — the opposite of whatever he, Jeff, would do in any given moment.

Merely *knowing* what Jesus would do is never enough. What I longed for was to become the kind of person who deeply loved the outcasts and freed those whom other people chained up — as Jesus did. I wanted to be kindhearted, authentic, and selfless, but I couldn't imagine this ever happening. I wanted to follow Jesus, but the trail seemed impassable. I wanted to take up my cross and follow . . . well, I wasn't sure I really wanted to do *that*.

Certain truths were dead to me: Living an eternal kind of life is possible here and now; traveling the journey of transformation toward Christlikeness is realistic; connecting with God could not only change me but bring that oneness with God described in Scripture. I now see that I was only half-alive.

AN ETERNAL KIND OF LIFE NOW

Most people view eternal life simply as existence that starts when you die and never ends. In reality, eternal (*aionios*) life begins now and refers not only to *length* of life but also the *quality* of life in which we experience wholeness and union with God. In such a life, we "experience here and now something of the splendour, and the majesty, and the joy, and the peace, and the holiness which are characteristic of the life of God."[1] An eternal kind of life is one of tasting daily the love of God — a love that "is a *divine life*, an *infinite energy*, an *irresistible power*"[2] that you and I are invited to participate in (see 2 Peter 1:3-4). It is "Christ *in you*, the hope of glory" (Colossians 1:27, italics added). It is "nothing else than the life of God himself" in you.[3]

Jesus defined eternal life this way: "Now this is eternal life: that they may *know you*, the only true God, and Jesus Christ, whom you have sent" (John 17:3, italics added). These days "knowing Christ" is often restricted to being able to say, "I believe that Jesus is the Christ, the Son of the living God." But the word *knowledge* (*ginosko*) as Jesus used it in John 17:3 "doesn't mean a mere acquaintance with facts nor an intellectual acceptance"; instead, it means "a complete devotion of the life in harmony with the revealed will of God and an intimate fellowship with Jesus."[4] It is not just mental assent to Jesus' divinity. It refers to personal fellowship.[5] God wants to have an *interactive relationship* with us. This personal interaction is what we see people in the Bible experiencing: God surrounding humans with hidden protection, God coming alongside them in battle, God wanting to hold their hand, and God initiating good things in people's lives, including correction (see 2 Kings 6:17; 2 Chronicles 20:17; Isaiah 42:6; Nehemiah 9).

God fervently desires to have this interactive knowledge with us: "I will give them a heart to *know* me, that I am the LORD. They will be my people, and I will be their God, for they will return to me with all their heart" (Jeremiah 24:7, italics added). The Hebrew word for "know," *yada*, is "more than intellectual, emotional knowledge, [but] to enter into deep commitment so profound that Yahweh *enters our experience with us*."[6] Jeremiah knew God this way: "Yet you *know* me, O LORD; you see me and test my thoughts about you" (Jeremiah 12:3, italics added).

Our relationship with God moves far beyond any human relationship, similar to but even more in depth than what ancients called a soul-friend relationship, in which "two hearts are united in one."[7] While such earthly soul-friendships are rooted in God, God invites us beyond this into a transforming, soul-friend relationship with his[8] unseen self who "knows my inward unseen life, the life that I never show another, . . . below the levels plumbed by our most intimate friends."[9] We can build this transforming soul-friend relationship with God even as we live here on Planet Earth because we were "made for heaven"[10] after all. This friendship with God is what we've been looking for all our lives.

Compare such richness with the now-prevalent "spirituality of *me, here,* and *now.* Self-centeredness, self-preoccupation, self-preservation. These familiar dynamics haunt many families and places of work, many church groups. The destruction is everywhere to be seen. . . . Self-interest is the operative ethic. . . . The point of one's life is the maintenance and refurbishing of oneself"[11] — diet and exercise, health and happiness for my family and me, becoming a better Christian, self-improving my way to heaven.

By contrast, Jesus taught us that it's not just *me*, but God and God's kingdom; it's not just *here*, but the world God "so loves"; it's not just *now*, but the communion of the saints throughout history, including wise ones of the past and those we need to build for in the future (see John 17:20-26).

TRANSFORMATION IS POSSIBLE

Because this life of union with God is available, we are not doomed "to live in Romans 7," as a colleague once grumbled to me. He quoted verse 15 to describe the state of his soul: "'I do not understand what I do. For what I want to do I do not do, but *what I hate I do*'" (italics added). For this fair and wise businessman, it was shocking to think we can live in Romans 8 — living in terms of the Spirit and having our minds full of what the Spirit desires (see verses 5-6).

Jesus described how obedient, transformed behavior naturally flows from a life of abiding in the vine: "Abide in me as I abide in you" (John 15:4, NRSV). That mutual indwelling provides us with the juices to bear fruit such as love, joy, and peace (see verse 5). But without such nourishment, we as branches wither and die (see verse 6). Abiding in Christ's love, however, creates obedience (see verses 9-10) because deep devotion to Jesus gives us the desire to obey and sustains us when we might otherwise have second thoughts. This abiding life of "absolute dependence and perfect confidence" occurs because "a branch . . . is of the very same nature as the vine, and has one life and one spirit with it."[12] Andrew Murray warned of the "unspeakable danger of our giving ourselves to work for God, and to bear fruit, with but little of the true abiding, the wholehearted losing of ourselves in Christ and His life."[13]

As we abide in Christ, we find ourselves more and more able to live in the power of the invisible kingdom of God, to become people who

- Live with joy and gratefulness
- Bless enemies (difficult people)
- Don't hold grudges
- Are not resentful
- Care deeply about others
- Don't run off at the mouth, but offer caring words
- Go the extra mile
- Live with purposeful intentionality
- Are humble (letting go of pride, not grabbing the credit or engaging in power struggles)
- Never, ever judge (that's God's job) (Matthew 5–7)

This kingdom life is the "life from above" of which Jesus spoke (John 3:31). It is lived in conversational relationship with God in which we "nourish ourselves on the person of God."[14] This journey of connecting with God, abiding in Christ, and living in terms of the Spirit is what we might call "soul school." It causes us to change inwardly, which is the key. We have problems with obedience when we try to change our outward behavior only, because we need to be transformed in our hearts. Trying to do good things that good people are supposed to do is misguided. God helps us change on the heart level because we behave according to what's in our hearts. The inner life of the soul must be transformed so we "become the *kind of person* from whom good deeds naturally flow"[15] rather than trying to be good and do everything right. Discipleship is not about going through a class or completing a course (though those may help). It's about letting the Spirit form in you a good heart that is devoted to God (see Galatians 4:19) so that you follow Jesus with great joy.

How does a change of heart occur? We increasingly have

interactive, face-to-face encounters with God: moments of conviction, moments of truth quietly spoken to us, moments of clarity ("Okay, now I get it!"), and moments of comfort and encouragement. In these moments we connect with God and learn to live a lifetime of such moments.

CONNECTING WITH GOD

To facilitate this life with God, we become willing to do whatever we need to do to connect with God in the next ten minutes — even if it looks very different from what the people around us do or what has been described in a book. As we connect with God, we change.

For example, when I first began volunteering at the Samaritan Center, a drop-in center for the homeless, I worked well with the clients except when they yelled at me or were sarcastic.

Then I snapped back. I felt terrible because I was supposed to be serving them. I finally forced myself to stop snapping back, but I kept thinking hot retorts in my mind, and these leaked into my facial expressions and tone of voice. Once when holding back an angry reply, I found myself saying, "I was only trying to be polite." The client responded, "Yes, that's very obvious. You were only *trying*." It hurt because he was right.

Finally it occurred to me to implement the spiritual discipline that is most basic to my journey with Jesus because I learned it when my children were small: practicing the presence of God.[16] So as I folded towels, I prayed for the clients around me, remembering situations and issues they'd confided in me. As I handed towels to clients, I greeted them by name and prayed for them. As I did laundry, I imitated Brother Lawrence, who was happy to pick up a piece of straw for the love of God.[17] Because my mind was filled with concern for the clients, I stopped taking things so personally.

Then one morning a few years ago, I saw clearly how it worked. I noticed that Donna, one of the clients, had two black eyes, and then

I found out that Tessa[18] had beaten her up. As I stood at the counter doing paperwork, two hands slammed down on the surface across from me. I looked up: It was Tessa. She was mad. She began telling me off about a certain procedure she didn't like. As I looked at her, I practiced God's presence by praying this breath prayer: "Show me this person's heart." When she said all the clients thought I was rude, I almost protested — they tell me I'm the most fun volunteer! But I stayed quiet, trying to see her heart. Finally, Tessa paused, quieted herself, and whispered that she knew the other clients were mad at her because of "what happened with Donna. So I decided that when I came in here to talk to you, I would be calm. I wouldn't get mad."

Immediately I patted her hands and replied, "You're doing a good job, Tessa. You're speaking very quietly and staying calm. Keep it up."

She grinned at me and said, "I thought so." I'd seen her heart — someone working on her temper — and so I could encourage her.

A little later, I reflected that I must be nuts. How could I encourage someone who had yelled at me? What had come over me? But I saw that the Holy Spirit had been working in me as I connected with God by practicing God's presence. *Let it alone*, I told myself. *It was a beautiful thing.* In fact, I had unintentionally blessed my enemy (a difficult person). A very different me finally stood behind that counter than the one who had begun volunteering years before.

In the beginning kindness seemed impossible. But following my longtime spiritual practice helped me connect with God, which caused compassion and kindness to flow better than before. When we put our effort into *whatever it takes to help us connect with God*, we quite naturally do good things without thinking about them. In such "accidental obedience," we obey out of a personal connection with God, not because we ordered ourselves to do it. That's how life with God works: You do the connecting (with God), and God does the perfecting (in your behavior).

The distinction of where to put the effort is crucial: not in trying to be good (or do what Jesus did) but in connecting with Jesus himself. A seminary student once explained to me his confusion that weekly chapel speakers seemed to contradict one another. One week someone pleaded, "Try really hard to be good." The next week another urged, "Let go and let God." He wondered, *Which is it?* He said to me, "Now I get it. I ask God about what practices I might do to connect with God and then I put my effort into doing those practices. Then I let go and let the Spirit work in me."

When we cooperate with God this way, we know it's not about us because it's so clearly *God's work* in us (see Philippians 1:6). C. S. Lewis described this process when he said that God doesn't love us because we're good, but because God loves us, God *makes us good.*[19] That changed heart is the Spirit's work in us, making us good in the moments we least expect it. Goodness flows because we're abiding in the Vine.

Moments of connecting are more likely to occur as we practice spiritual disciplines or exercises (such as practicing the presence of God). These practices are described in the Bible, especially in the behavior of Jesus. The key word is "practice." They're intensified moves, such as playing scales on the piano or practicing a serve in tennis. We do the same movements over and over behind the scenes when no one is watching. Then when it's time to play the piano in a recital or serve a tennis ball in a match, the fingers or arm flies with precision. In the meantime, spiritual practices help us stay in the flow of the Spirit so that we live an interactive life with God.

The catch is that we must first *become willing* to do whatever we need to do to connect with God. Sentimental longing will not do; we have to want it more than we want anything else. When we decide to become a disciple of Jesus — to be his apprentice in all matters of life — we also decide to set aside many other wonderful things, much to other people's dismay. We become like that pearl merchant working online all night until she finds that perfect pearl she's been seeking. Then she sells the house, the car, the boat, even her bed, and rearranges her whole life to purchase this treasure (see Matthew 13:45-46). Everything is set aside to respond to that invitation: "Follow me."

THIS BOOK AS "A CURRICULUM FOR CHRISTLIKENESS"[20]

This book does not focus on helping you to change your behaviors or to practice spiritual disciplines, but it places Jesus in the center of your vision and lets Jesus lead you into this eternal kind of life. In each chapter of this book, I present a characteristic of Jesus that we often overlook or take for granted, yet when we examine Jesus this way we are astonished and drawn to him. We also explore these aspects in today's terms: How would Jesus live his life today if he had my life as a journalist, a computer tech, a hairstylist, a school crossing guard, a CEO of a start up company? At the end of each chapter, I suggest experiments for connecting with God — spiritual practices you might use (as the Holy Spirit leads) to follow Jesus into this way of being. You, no doubt, might have many others to suggest. As you review the suggested practices (specific versions of spiritual disciplines), consider these cautions:

Disciplines are not just for elite Christians. Everybody performs disciplines, but they don't call them that. For example, many people employ the discipline of "study" for shopping. My friend "studies" bargains, and so she informed me that a popular restaurant puts its premium pies on sale twice a year: February and October. I benefit from her discipline of "study."

Disciplines are not necessarily heroic. Disciplines work best when they fit within the ordinary fabric of our everyday lives. For example, I noticed many years ago that I complained about people a lot. So I made a decision that every time I complained about someone out loud or in my mind, I would pause and pray for the person. Usually I prayed something along the lines of Philippians 3:10 — that they would "know Christ" in a deeper way. Eventually I skipped the complaint and went right to the prayer. It was no big deal — just a few seconds now and then.

Motives matter. It's easy to do spiritual practices for the wrong reasons, especially to be a better Christian or to be holy. The goal of doing a spiritual discipline is to help you *connect* with God — abide in Christ, live in terms of the Spirit. This union with God then transforms you into Christlikeness. Doing these disciplines equips you to love God and love your neighbor (the Great Commandment). As you "train yourself to be godly," you "share in the life of Christ"[21] (1 Timothy 4:7).

But focus and motives easily go astray. For example, as some people read the Bible every day, they become eager to check off that task to get it done or because they hope it will help them have a better day. Such motives cause them to read the Bible primarily to finish the task. But if their goal in reading is to connect with God, they won't focus on getting to the bottom of the page. They take time to pause in the middle because they sense God speaking to them. As they linger over the text — maybe even every day for a week — they find themselves doing the good things mentioned in the passage without even realizing it. Because they are abiding, they bear fruit and obey. The more they bear fruit and obey, the more they want to abide.

Forget What You Think You Know . . .

As you read each chapter, it may help if you decide now that you're willing to take a fresh look at Jesus, which may mean you need to set aside certain preconceived ideas. N. T. Wright warned us, "Don't come with a set fixed idea of who God is, and try to fit Jesus into that. *Look at Jesus*, the Jesus who wept at the tomb of a friend, the one who washed his followers' feet, and you'll see who is the true God."[22] The Jesus you meet in the Gospels is your best clue about what God is like. By saying, "Anyone who has seen me has seen the Father" (John 14:9), Jesus was telling us to "forget everything we think we know about the nature of God and lose ourselves in this picture of our Father."[23]

May you find great joy in your vision of life with Jesus in the kingdom of God.

QUESTIONS FOR DISCUSSION AND REFLECTION

1. Read again the list of phrases that describes life in the kingdom of God (under "Transformation Is Possible"). Choose a word that describes what it would feel like to live such a life.
2. What would be the best thing about oneness with Christ (union with God)?
3. When have you had an interactive, face-to-face encounter with God? What was it like? If you've never had that experience, what do you think it might be like?
4. In what area(s) of your life would you like to see genuine change?

❧

1. Living a life of purpose
   Peace w/ God
2. Letting go & letting the Spirit work in & through me.
3. Knowing / God spoke to me.
4. Judgement of others
   True care / love for others

Part 1

JESUS, THE RELATER-
STYLE SAVIOR

2   God *with* Us

The woman's words stirred me, as did the glowing look on her face. As a lifelong good-deed doer who had always tried hard to be good enough, she heard a different message from Jesus. As she had meditated on John 15, a phrase in verse 15 stood out to her. She spoke it to me, her spiritual director, just above a whisper: "Jesus told me, 'I call you friend.'" She continued, "I'm no longer just a servant. I really am his friend!" In the midst of this bonding moment with Jesus, she began to release a difficult family situation she'd been trying to control for years. Such is the dramatic effect of friendship with Jesus: She did the connecting with God, and God was doing the perfecting in her.

For God to choose to call human beings "friends" is a radical thought. We're as shocked by this as was the junior devil, Wormwood, in *The Screwtape Letters* when his uncle Screwtape explained that God "*really* loves the hairless bipeds."[1] I can picture the furrowed eyebrows of Wormwood and Screwtape as they wonder, *How could that be?* We too wonder, *How could God really love us, even like us, and invite us to be friends?*

NEVER MECHANICAL, ALWAYS RELATIONAL

Too often we frame God's invitation to share in his life as a contract (If I do A, God will do B) and we miss out on the real thing — the life of God's own self. In this legal, mechanical approach, we view God as a vending machine. Into the slot we insert our coins (good deeds, church activities) and put our hand out waiting for the rewards to drop (answered prayers, a life free of major problems). But when life circumstances become bleak (especially compared with someone next door who doesn't profess faith), we become disappointed, even kicking the vending machine and grumbling, "Why didn't I get what I prayed for?"

The dark truth is that in this mechanical view of God's ways, we are not loving God but using God. We seek God's blessings instead of God's own self. We make use of God only to find solutions to problems, not to embrace God as the daily companion of our soul. In the mechanical view, we are like children attending boarding school who write letters home every week asking for money because parents are primarily sources of money. In the relational view of God, we are like children who work alongside Mom and Dad all day. We experience ups and downs together, tell jokes, and even share a few secrets. When we need something, we simply ask our parents. But without that soul-friend relationship with God, prayer becomes an attempt to manipulate God, who must be appeased.

Jesus would have none of this mechanical approach to God but insisted on a relationship of mutual abiding, saying, Live in union with me; abide *in* me as I abide *in* you. Those answered prayers so firmly sought in the mechanical view of God become a natural part of mutual abiding: "Ask whatever you wish, and it will be given you" (John 15:7).

Jesus didn't speak of a "plan of salvation" because he was the *person* of salvation (see John 14:6; 17:3). Lewis commented, "The things [Jesus] says are very different from what any other teacher has said. Others say, 'This is the truth about the Universe. This is the way you ought to go,' but He says, 'I am the Truth, and the Way, and the Life.' He says, 'No man can reach absolute reality, except through Me. . . . Eat Me, drink Me, I am your Food.'"[2]

THE COMMUNITY OF THE TRINITY

Jesus' relational nature doesn't surprise us when we consider that he is one of a three-person community of love. Clark Pinnock explained, "Love flows among the persons of the Godhead. . . . It is the essence of God's nature to be relational. . . . God is pure ecstasy — each Person exists in loving relationship with the other Persons. . . . The Trinity is a fellowship of giving and receiving."[3]

No competition, hierarchy, or vying for power exists within the Trinity. Instead they give away power: The Father is not afraid to place everything in the Son's hands (see John 3:35). The Spirit is given "without limit" with no fear that the Spirit will take over (John 3:34). God is not threatened by giving Jesus the highest place and a name above his own (see Philippians 2:9). These "three distinct Persons live together in full, unchallenged equality, glad submission to each other [and] joyful intimacy with each other."[4]

Relating in such community is the eternal kind of life we were built for. It is the way God has designed the world: God and Christ and the Holy Spirit living in oneness and enlarging their circle to draw us in so that we live in union with them and then love one another (see John 15:9-12; 17:20-21).

To enlarge that circle, God created us for relationship, as evidenced by how Jesus chose his disciples to "be with" him. Besides teaching and learning, they did a lot of hanging out — eating together, traveling together, playing together. (What sort of horseplay occurred on those other-side-of-the-lake excursions? Leg wrestling? First-century football? Samaritan soccer?) When the disciples agonized over how they would manage without Jesus, he assured them, "I will *come back* and *take you to be with me* that *you also may be where I am*" (John 14:3, italics added; see also 15:3,16; 17:24). Then Jesus reassured them that the Counselor is *"to be with you* forever" (John 14:16, italics added). Later, Jesus' parting words to the band of followers, "I am *with you* always" reveal that "having him *with* them is their whole reason for being who they are."[5]

JESUS' RELATIONAL METHODS

As we embrace and teach the relational *message* of Jesus, we need to embrace the relational *methods* of Jesus.[6] He treated people as distinct individuals instead of assembly-line workers. No two healings were alike because Jesus looked inside each troubled person and then did or said what was needed to enlarge the individual's faith whether he or she was an outcast leper or a royal official. Only once (that we know of) did he

- Interrupt a funeral to talk to the corpse (Luke 7:11-16)
- Quiz someone seeking help: "Do you believe that I am able to do this?" (Matthew 9:28)
- Deem it necessary to forgive someone's sins before healing him (Mark 2:5)
- Spar verbally with someone so as to evoke from her a deep understanding of God's grace (Mark 7:24-30)
- Pantomime the entire healing as an outward enactment of the movement of unseen power whizzing around this deaf person. Reenact this. Jesus would have been cradling his face. (Mark 7:31-37)
- Have a support-group style conversation with the parent of the one he healed: "How long has he been like this?" (Mark 9:21)
- Challenge an infirm person: "Do you *want* to get well?" (John 5:6, italics added)

Each person needed something different to trust Jesus more deeply, so he looked deeply within each person and worked with those needs. This is the only way we can ever be of help to anyone as well. He will help us see what people really need.

Jesus didn't use clinical, one-size-fits-all methods as we do — establishing policies, inventing programs, and printing manuals (this being the more efficient way of doing things). One time a church's women's ministry team asked me to suggest a policy for giving baby showers to unmarried pregnant women. (They wanted to help these girls but did not want to seem to condone sex outside of marriage.) After finding out the first girl's name, I asked about her financial situation, her relationships with people at church, her parents' feelings, and so on. "Does she need a baby shower or does she need something else?" I asked them. The team members didn't know the answers to these questions and decided to meet with this young woman to discern the answers. When I asked for the second woman's name, the leader asked, "Are you going to ask these questions about every girl?" I knew Jesus would. They stepped up to the plate with three of them forming a team to visit each girl to listen to her and find out what she needed. "Not a policy, but the person," they told me.

Jesus' focus on people probably startled the disciples over and over. They wanted to ignore kids; he wanted to bless them. They wanted the blind beggar to stop yelling and following them; Jesus stopped in his tracks and asked Bartimaeus what he wanted done for him. They would never have spoken to an immoral Samaritan woman; he asked her for help and held a conversation with her in front of everyone (see Matthew 19:13-14; Mark 10:51; John 4:7). Never a hit-and-run healer, Jesus routinely paused to have restorative conversations with people such as the man born blind and the woman with the flow of blood. People and their stories mattered to Jesus. Even now, Jesus invests in people and is eager to interact with us.

Ever the relater, Jesus had an invitational nature that abounded, telling all sorts of people in all sorts of places to *come* to him (see

Matthew 4:19; 11:28; Mark 6:31; 10:14; John 7:37; 21:12). When those early disciples asked him, "Where are you staying?" he did not reply (as I would have), "Why do you want to know?" Instead Jesus said, "Come and see" (John 1:38-39, NRSV). Ever the party giver (see Luke 15:2,6,9,23), Jesus portrayed the kingdom of God as a luxurious feast to which he continually invites us (see Matthew 8:11; 22:2-9; 25:10; Luke 12:36; 14:15-24; 15:23). Today Jesus perpetually invites us to the Supper of the Lord to be with him and take him in.

Encountering Jesus

Jesus continually pulled people outside time and space to encounter his otherworldly self (see John 4:26; 9:37). In never-to-be-forgotten *kairos* moments, when time must have seemed to stand still, he reached out to people and engaged them, often calling them by name. To the grieving, perplexed Mary Magdalene in the garden of his tomb, Jesus simply said her name and she suddenly knew him (see John 20:16). To the fierce, much-mistaken Saul of Tarsus, Jesus did not send a message saying, "Your doctrine needs correction. Go back to rabbinical school, restudy the Messiah passages, and you'll see that Jesus is Lord." Instead Jesus appeared to him personally and demanded, "Saul, Saul, why are *you* persecuting *Me*?" and, "*I* am Jesus whom *you* are persecuting" (Acts 9:4-5, NASB, italics added).

Jesus, as God with skin on, touched people. His hands enfleshed the love of God: scooping up healed children and handing them back to their grieving parents; cradling his disciples' feet; touching the eyes of blind men; helping up those he healed (see Luke 7:11-16; 9:42; John 13:5; Matthew 9:29; 9:25). When we might expect those hands to have been fisted in anger during his arrest, Jesus reached them out to heal the ear of his opponent's slave (see Luke 22:51).

Consider what it would have been like for each of these people he touched. One blind man's first object of sight was Jesus-the-carpenter's muscular, tool-wielding fingers over his eyes. In between those fingers he then saw the intense look on Jesus' face as he released his power (see Mark 8:22-26). As each healed person went to sleep that night (and perhaps every night for the rest of their lives), they could imagine Jesus' face and touch all over again, knowing they would never be the same.

Jesus and "the Look"

Lovers fix their eyes on one another with sustained interest; parents and children often gaze at each other. Sometimes I can't take my eyes off my son or daughter even though they're adults. And they want that gaze. When our daughter waited on tables at a restaurant, we would go to eat there and catch her peeking at us from across the room to make sure we watched how hard she worked. She was asking, *Mom and Dad, please look at me!* People long for the searching gaze of another person to rest on them, especially the gaze of those who are significant to them.

Knowing this, of course, Jesus often locked eyes with people, using intense looks. After Peter's third denial of any acquaintance with Jesus (this would be like your mother telling a courtroom of people she'd never seen you before), Jesus — while standing in the high priest's courtyard — maneuvered himself into a position where he turned "and *looked straight* at Peter" (Luke 22:61, italics added). Based on Jesus' character, we can guess that the expression on his face was not one that said, *I told you so* (the look of an arrogant know-it-all) or, *Look what you've done to me* (the look of a codependent victim). Those postures are so much a part of us but not a part of him. His look probably matched his previous warning words to Peter about the denials and so would have urged, *Don't let your faith fail. Turn back and strengthen your brothers!* (see Luke 22:31-32).

Letting this urgent look penetrate our soul helps us connect with Jesus when we make mistakes. Will I turn to Christ so my faith doesn't fail? Will I strengthen the people around me? Neither Jesus nor the angels are shocked when I fail. The crucial issue is not to agonize over failures but to turn to Christ in faith in the midst of them.

When we allow ourselves to enter into encounters with Jesus this way, we begin to take Jesus' confidence in us seriously — much more seriously than we take our own fragile attempts to be good. Our faith becomes about Jesus, not about us.

The Look of Love

Imagine yourself as an eager young know-it-all who has come up with a penetrating question to ask the intriguing itinerant preacher Jesus (see Matthew 19:16-22; Mark 10:17-22). You, first in your seminary class, admire this teacher, so you run up to him, and in the manner customary to your culture, you fall on your knees in front of him as any prospective disciple would do. Then you present this question: "Good teacher, what must I do to inherit eternal life?" (You and fellow students have spent hours arguing that question.)

Instead of lauding you for your earnest spirituality, Jesus questions your use of the word *good*. He alludes to how this word should be used to describe only God. You think, *A word study! I knew he was brilliant.* Then Jesus quotes the commandments you've known since you could walk and talk. You assure him you've obeyed them.

Then comes the moment you will never forget: Jesus *looks at you and loves you*. What does such an expression look like? Try shutting your eyes and fixing his facial expression in your imagination. How would it affect you to be gazed upon and loved so well?

As you steady yourself to absorb such full-hearted love, Jesus says what you least expect to hear: "One thing you lack. Go, sell everything you have and give to the poor, and you will have treasure in heaven. Then come, follow me" (Mark 10:21).

How could Jesus demand that you give up your fortune — which is, after all, what makes you who you are? How does he know this? Maybe you now want him to stop looking at you with love, because you can't receive this truth about yourself. Perhaps you've never heard piercing reality spoken with such great love. This is too much. Everything inside you collapses and you walk away sad.

Sit for a moment in this scene and absorb it. All of us have resisted truth at one time or another. Are you willing to let Jesus speak to you truth that will give you a "life that is life indeed"?

To Experience This Look

I began experiencing this loving look from Jesus more than twenty years ago when I first noticed he "looked at him and loved him," but the next phrase ("Go, sell . . .") scared me. In the previous months, God had prodded me to give up certain eating-related behaviors. I tried reading books, but they didn't help me. I sensed Jesus was asking me to go to a 12-step group (through a friend of mine), but I was too proud. As I entered into the passage yet another time, I saw that like the rich young ruler I turned away from Jesus' instruction, but unlike him I kept doing it every day.

Then in the worst season of my life — marriage falling apart, church-related job falling away, fear of losing everything — I sat in desperate prayer, and it seemed that Jesus was looking at me and loving me, asking me one more time to go to a meeting. That warm, inviting face said, "Give up what is precious to you — your pride, your childhood habits of using food for comfort — and come back and be my disciple." I called my friend and agreed to go to a meeting. She and I went every week for years, and there I found the relational healing I so desperately needed. I could not be healed by reading a book. I needed people. I came to understand then that transformation into Christlikeness is done mostly through relationship.

Through the years, this scene between Jesus and me has occurred over and over about all sorts of things. I sense Jesus coming to me, head tilted to one side, and saying, "How 'bout it, girl? Will you give it up?" At times, I've said, "This is a joke, right? Me give up ____?" While his look is never scolding, it is almost too much to bear. But it makes me ponder what it would look like to do what he's inviting me to do. It never becomes easy, just less difficult.

The more we allow Jesus to look at us and love us, the more we trust Jesus and are drawn to him. We increasingly understand that Jesus is a glimpse of the Father, who gazes deeply at us — who can't take his eyes off us (see Song of Songs 2:4, MSG).

THE PERSONAL GOD WHO LOVES

Understanding this personal approach of Jesus helps us embrace a relational view of God. Think of the difference it makes in your life whether you see God issuing orders or inviting, wooing, and drawing. This relational view is based on our truly believing God *wants us* and wants to be our companion. Most of us doubt — deep down — that God loves us. Almost in jest (where truth is frequently revealed), people say horrible things such as, "God slapped me upside the head this week when . . ." or "Just when I thought I knew which end was up, God pulled the rug out from under me." Really? God is not an abusive trickster, nor was Jesus. God treasures the self we keep hidden and wants to transform that self into the person we'd love to be.

This truth is so all-encompassing that it may take an entire lifetime of connecting with God to get it. For now we keep moving in that direction. As we do, we feel more and more of that deep sense of okay-ness that satisfies these searching questions: Who will I let peer into the eyes of my soul? Who will I trust with things I've never told anyone? Who will treat my soul with the respect and tenderness it needs? This comes only from a soul-friend relationship with God and the people whom God supplies.

As you read the practices that follow, do so prayerfully. Then consider if God is inviting you to experiment with any of them. If so, feel free to tweak them. (To become absorbed in the techniques of any discipline is to kill its connection with God.) Use them to let your soul become enthralled with the kingdom of God and meet Jesus in the midst of them.

EXPERIMENTS IN CONNECTING WITH GOD
(Spiritual Practices to Consider)

To RECEIVE this relational invitation from God

Celebration: Participate in Communion (Eucharist) with the idea that Jesus invites you to take in his own self. If your own church doesn't offer Communion soon, visit another and consider that the strangers around you are not strangers to Jesus or to others in the kingdom of God.

Fellowship: Interact regularly with someone who knows how to look you in the eye and love you, who believes in you. Practice responding to that person in the same way.

Meditation: Read Mark 10:17-31 and picture it happening. Write down the feelings you would have had if you had been the rich young ruler. Jot down anything else about Jesus that comes to you.

Meditation: Read Zephaniah 3:17 and picture yourself being sung over by God, being quieted with God's love.

Meditation: Read John 17:20-26. Focus especially on verse 21. Picture the Trinity sitting in a circle, eager to draw you into the middle of their circle, enfolding you.

Prayer: Give God permission to say difficult truths to you, promising you won't beat yourself up but put your trust in God.

Recollection and prayer: Think back over your life. What have been your *kairos* moments with God? What happened between you and God? Thank God for these moments and ask for continued clarity.

Reflection: What truth are you finding difficult to hear? Know that Jesus looks at you and loves you while he says it to you.

Study and meditation: Look for Old Testament passages in which "being with" God is central. (See Psalm 23:4; Isaiah 43:2;

Genesis 26:3 to get started.) Which one resonates most with you?

Worship: Read the words to the hymn "Come, Thou Fount." Relish the second verse about Jesus seeking you out while you were a stranger. Sing this out to God, thankful for that searching gaze.

To BECOME one who offers the relational life of Jesus to others

Fellowship: Consider how you interact with people through looks and touch and calling people by name. How might you do these things in such a way to invest in people?

Practicing the presence of God: As you talk to people, pray for them. This will probably cause you to look intently at them.

Silence: When someone speaks to you, look intently at the person and receive what he or she is saying with quietness.

Service: Consider how you serve in a mechanical way. How do you need to be more relational in your service?

Service: Pray for each person you serve, asking God to show you his or her needs.

Study: As people speak, study them. Notice how they stand, hold their arms, and move their eyebrows. Ask God, *What's going on inside this person that I need to know about? How can I serve this person?*

QUESTIONS FOR DISCUSSION AND REFLECTION

1. Consider the instances listed under "Jesus' Relational Methods." How would it feel to have Jesus look inside you and enlarge your faith?

2. What look do you ascribe to the face of God in those moments when you feel convicted? Schoolmarmish? Annoyed? Disappointed? Encouraging? What look most accurately reflects the heart of God?

3. On a scale of 1 to 10, how safe do you feel with God (1: completely unsafe; 10: completely safe)? On a scale of 1 to 10, how certain do you feel that God loves you and wants to be with you (1: completely unsure; 10: sure)? If you're willing, tell why you gave your answer.
4. What does this chapter lead you to want to pray?
5. Which of the above experiments do you see yourself trying out this week?

1. I would love for Him to enlarge my faith, but to see me all tho I know He does makes me sad.

2. I know He looks at me with true + unconditional love, but I don't look at myself the same way.
• The Lack of Love!

3. 8, 10 - I am hard on me so I feel God feels the same.

4. next pg.

5. to love me as God loves me

3 Attentive Listener

How do you feel when someone speaks to you but doesn't look at you? Perhaps coworkers continue working at their task or fidgeting with whatever's in front of them. Or someone asks you a question but keeps talking without waiting for you to answer. Or you're at a conference where people don't look at each other when they talk because they're looking for someone else they may want to talk to. Or at church "greeting times" you find the emphasis is on greeting as many people as possible without ever locking eyes with others and offering them the love of Jesus. Such inattentiveness makes it clear that people and relationships are not important — or not as important as getting things done.

I confess that I have been this inattentive person. In these scenarios, I have too much to think about and too much to do. One of my soul-schoolrooms of retraining was when my kids were teens and would come into my office to talk to me. I didn't want to stop working! It would take an imaginary crane to pull my eyes away from the computer screen and turn my entire body toward that precious person standing next to me. To look at my teen meant that he or she was uppermost in my mind. I had to work hard to learn to honor these dear conversation partners.

Dietrich Bonhoeffer described this "half-listening" phenomenon: "There is a kind of listening with half an ear that presumes already to know what the other person has to say. It is an impatient, inattentive listening, that despises the brother and is only waiting for a chance to speak and thus get rid of the other person."[1] Perhaps it seems too harsh to say that to listen inattentively is to *despise* a person. But despising someone is the opposite of respecting him or her, and respect is a core expression of love.

Equally dishonoring is the habit of interrupting. I would never interrupt someone I respect enormously, but I'd do it to a friend. When I interrupt people, I'm telling them that what they're saying to me doesn't matter. Or it doesn't matter as much as what I want to say. What matters most is that I want to talk.

To live an eternal kind of life in the kingdom of God is to treat others with love and respect. How do we change? How is transformation made possible? As we implement little practices that teach us to love more and listen more, it helps to regularly experience Jesus, the Living Word, who is focused on us and listens to us here and now. One way to do this is to crawl into the skin of someone Jesus encountered by immersing ourselves in a situation described in Scripture. Then we can receive from Jesus that rapt attention that they received from him.

FOCUSED ATTENTION

One such encounter is Jesus' interaction with the woman who was hemorrhaging (see Mark 5:24-34). First, move into this woman's world, imagining the disease's effect on her body and mind. (Men may want to recast the story as a man with a putrid oozing sore that creates a mess and must be cleaned out regularly.) Your disease is so abhorrent that no one is allowed to touch you. That means you have not been patted on the shoulder (much less hugged) for twelve years. Also, you stink. People don't like to be around you and they joke about you behind your back. Your house has an odor. Maybe your children have stopped coming to visit. (Someone whose mother had a similar disease told me she couldn't stand to go into her mother's bedroom.) Maybe *you* don't like to be around you. As a person of wealth and dignity (before you spent all your money on doctors who were unable to help), you have been forced to live a lonely existence.

But you've heard about a new prophet — Jesus of Nazareth — who often stays in Capernaum, where you live. He has already healed several people in your town (see 1:21-34; 3:1-6). After he healed Peter the fisherman's mother-in-law, crowds of sick people came to their door and he healed all of them, but you obviously did not get in line. You'd like to approach him now, but there are so many reasons you can't. (If you're the woman, you should not speak to a teacher in public.) Any contact with you as a diseased person would make Jesus ceremonially unclean and unable to teach. That would be wrong — he's such a good teacher. So you devise a plan.

You watch Jesus as he comes ashore from a boat and you follow him. (To say that you "stalked" him mistakes your motives but describes your movements.) You can't touch him, but what about his clothes? It sounds superstitious, but perhaps his power rubs onto his clothes. You manage to go unnoticed into the crowd and see how the fringe of the shoulder-draped mantle that teachers wear drags on the ground. So you touch it.

Immediately you feel in your body that you are healed. Sit in that for a moment. The pain ceases. The flow or ooze stops, and whatever messiness that accompanied it disappears. The odor vanishes as well.

These physical changes take your breath away. You stop to breathe, while the crowd keeps moving with Jesus. But then Jesus stops. He knows when power leaves his body, and he wants to make contact with the recipient of that power. Why does he do this? Does he understand that your healing is still incomplete until you have interacted with him — that you also need relational healing from your isolation and shunning by others? He asks, "Who touched me?" and the disciples — understandably in a hurry to heal the little girl of an important synagogue official — become annoyed by Jesus' delay. His question seems as silly as a running back at the bottom of a football player pile-up asking who touched him. But Jesus is determined not to move on until he locks eyes with the cured one.

Do you want Jesus to find you? Perhaps not, because it would be embarrassing. You "stole" your healing, after all. But on the other hand, you want to thank this holy man. So you stand there — hoping he *won't* find you, but hoping he *will* find you. He could call out to you, but instead he honors your need to delay as you feel the sensations of a now-healed body. He does not rush you but waits until you're ready.

Finally, you can bear it no longer and you lunge forward and fall at his feet. There, you confess the "whole truth" (5:33), a rather shocking thing for you to do. What will people think of a woman describing her gynecological disorder in a crowd of devout Jewish men, or even a man telling his personal story this way? But Jesus does not stop you from your "talking cure." You tell your story and confess your truth.

Jesus doesn't interrupt your telling of the "whole truth" but instead patiently gazes at you, perhaps similarly to the way he looked at the rich young ruler and loved him. He doesn't seem to have anywhere to go. "For the moment, it seemed for Him no one but that woman and nothing but her need existed."[2] When you finish your story, Jesus says an outrageous, affectionate thing — he calls you by a term of childhood endearment: "daughter" (or "son" or "my dear child"). Then he announces to all (including people who have avoided you and made fun of you for years) that your trust in him counted. He says that *your faith* made you whole! You are now free to go in peace and be freed from your suffering. See Jesus' face as he says this to you.

A LISTENING LIFE IN A HURRIED WORLD

Jesus did not become an attentive listener by attending a communications skills seminar. This transforming practice flowed naturally from him because he didn't routinely move through life with an impatient, hurried heart. His attentive listening and undivided focus flowed from who he was inside. No matter who you were, you were never lost in the crowd to him. When he was with people, it was as though he was practicing *lectio divina* on them: reading them, reflecting on them, responding to them, even resting in who they were.[3] He listened for and commented on people's fears and their seeds of faith even though they weren't aware they had any faith at all.

Resist the urge to think that Jesus' attentive listening is a marginal thing—something he did because he was super-nice. This is how many people think of God—like themselves but bigger and nicer. While listening to others is a nice thing to do, this powerful tractor-beam gaze of Jesus' eyes radiated his beauty, truth, and power. This was nothing like you and I have ever experienced from anyone—no matter how nice that person may be.

For Jesus, listening was a vehicle to love people. He listened with love to the father of the demon-possessed boy who asked for help. Instead of immediately healing the boy, Jesus engaged him in conversation, asking him, "How long has [the boy] been like this?" (Mark 9:21). It was as if Jesus was having his own one-on-one support group for parents of sick kids, saying, "Tell me how bad it's been!" Jesus knew it would help the father to talk about it. This includes but is more than letting people get things "off their chest" or even "share their pain." Jesus gave this boy's father the gift of his weighty, healing presence.

While some teachers don't make good listeners, Jesus did. "Christians (especially ministers) so often think they must always contribute something when they are in the company of others, that this is the one service they have to render. They forget that listening can be a greater *service* than speaking."[4] How is listening *serving*? Consider that the most basic movements of service are to look (to see what's really going on inside people, to investigate their practical needs), to listen (to empty self of brilliant ideas and hear people express their needs), and to love (to sacrifice and offer what others most need).[5] When I feel overwhelmed by a task of service, I remind myself to go back to these basics: look, listen, and love.

I have to remind myself to bring this presence of Jesus — to look, listen, and love — when I serve on an Epiphany Ministry team conducting three-day retreats inside youth correctional facilities.[6] The teenage felons are sullen. We teach them and worship with them and eat table meals with them, but mostly we just hang out. We sing silly songs, do goofy skits, and play juvenile games together. It usually takes them a full day to warm up.

Like the bleeding woman, these kids are outcasts. Most have been rejected by their families and have nowhere to go. They receive mostly negative attention. While I use ministry skills there (teaching, small-group interaction, spiritual direction), they count for very little compared with listening to the kids and loving them. Twelve hours a day, three adults and five kids sit at each of the six tables, putting into practice this ministry's most strategic tactic: listen, listen, love, love. The kids know we'll hear whatever they say and not reject them. In time, they tell us things: how both of the teen's parents are in jail; how a grandfather is a serial rapist and what he did to this teen; or how the teen murdered the man who raped his baby sister. Occasionally, we also say things — we hope they're the right things. Most of all, we try to bring Jesus to those tables during that weekend and subsequent visits. Sometimes, the teens are "freed from [their] suffering" (Mark 5:34).

We watch many of them make turnarounds — different facial expressions, different thoughts, different goals — and move toward Christ. One boy said to me, "When I came, I thought there was nothing good left in me — nothing God could love. Now I know God loves me." Such transformation is possible because they have tasted life in the kingdom of God.

If we "consider carefully how [we] listen," hidden things are no longer concealed (Luke 8:17-18). Careful listening allows us to understand the hidden things about people and situations. It enables us to comprehend so much more than if we're distracted. We love the person more deeply, and when we do talk, fitting words flow from us.

LEARNING FROM THE LISTENER

Viewing Jesus as an attentive listener makes me want to follow him around forever. It makes me want to become his disciple — a learner, an apprentice — so I can hear from him continually and then turn that blessing around to others. Since servant-listening is as much caught as taught, we need to catch this capacity to listen directly from Jesus as we experience him listening to us.

Being Listened to By Jesus

This may happen while meditating on Scripture as we enter into the text. Sometimes it happens when someone preaches or speaks personally to you and you have a sense that God is talking directly to you. Overseas missionaries not infrequently give reports of Jesus appearing to people.

In a more natural way, it happens as we practice the presence of God and move in the rhythm of prayer all day long. As we spill our thoughts and feelings to Jesus, we become amazed that he never tires of us. He never looks around for a more important person. In that moment, we are heard; we matter.

As we are listened to by Jesus, we increasingly understand that this Jesus is a glimpse of the Father, and we come to understand that our God is one who listens deeply when we pray or cry out in trouble or jump for joy. There's no such thing as God being too busy for us.

Listening to Jesus

We aren't born knowing how to listen to God. We learn to do it just like lambs learn to recognize their shepherd's voice because "they spend most of the hours of most of the days with the shepherd"[7] (see John 10:27). Even today, Middle Eastern shepherds are familiar with each sheep's markings and personality, so they come into a crowded sheepfold and call the sheep by name, leading them out one by one. This is a picture of how we were designed to live — spending most of the hours of most of our days connecting with God, being spoken to by God, responding to God's voice, and following God's leading. Without this, we live in loneliness and uncertainty, always grasping for more. To listen to God requires experimentation and practice so that we develop "ears to hear" (Mark 4:9,23; Luke 7:18; 14:35). Such practice involves Scripture study and meditation, prayer (especially contemplative prayer), and paying attention to teaching as well as supposedly insignificant conversations.[8]

Listening to Others

From the experience of being listened to by Jesus, we take the kingdom of God to others, including this others-referenced way of being present to people and listening deeply to their souls' cries. We do our part in forming a community of prayerful love here on this earth that continues into eternity. Can you imagine such a community where people are present to each other this way?

To listen deeply can be a struggle because we have to let go of our agenda and the need to defend ourselves or the desire to persuade people to see things our way. (Sadly, this agenda-driven method describes some hit-and-run approaches to witnessing today. The all-important witnessing tool of listening has been forgotten.) When we set that aside and open our hearts to other people, it's amazing how we experience Christ-with-us loving them.

Following the example of a friend, I've attempted to practice a discipline of silence by not giving my opinion unless asked. When

I was teaching several nights at a church, I discovered the pastor's daughter was a painter. As an art history hobbyist, I asked who her favorite painter was. Even before she opened her lips to reply, I realized I was not listening for her answer. I asked her only because I wanted to tell her who my favorite painters were and offer a story about a piece of art I'd most recently become fascinated by. Recalling my intention not to offer my opinion until asked, I disciplined myself to listen fully to her.

After she responded, she didn't ask who my favorite painter was! So I asked her more questions. As she spilled out her thoughts, I could see more of her inner self. I marveled with joy at this teenager God had put in my life. I almost missed that moment of connection in my hurry to offer my opinion.

Listening is one of the most basic ways we submit to each other. In fact, listening is minute-by-minute submission to others. I clear away what's going on in my mind and I follow what others are saying. I "die" to my own desires and "live" to theirs.

Loving God and loving others are tied together. Said Dietrich Bonhoeffer, "He who can no longer listen to his brother will soon be no longer listening to God either; he will be doing nothing but prattle in the presence of God too. This is the beginning of the death of the spiritual life, and in the end there is nothing left but spiritual chatter."[9] But as we live life in union with God, we become steeped in empathy and genuinely care for other persons. We begin to live our lives in Jesus' attentive presence. This is what life in the kingdom of God here and now is meant to be.

EXPERIMENTS IN CONNECTING WITH GOD
(Spiritual Practices to Consider)

To RECEIVE this listening look from God

Fellowship: Interact with someone who listens to you without interrupting. Notice the peace and love you receive from this person. Practice responding to that person in the same way. Then venture out and try it with someone who normally interrupts you.

Meditation: Read Mark 5:24-34 and picture it happening. Write down the feelings you would have had if you had been this woman. Jot down anything else about Jesus that comes to you.

Prayer and silence: After praying, sit quietly for a few minutes. (Start with a few seconds.) You're not doing this to get God to speak to you. You're doing it to practice being quiet with God so that you will live a listening life all day long.

To BECOME one who listens deeply

If God leads you into one of the following disciplines, first picture yourself doing it in a few tough cases. If this makes you laugh, that's okay. Laughter is often a confession.

Chastity: Focus your eyes carefully on someone you find attractive and ask God, *What does this person need from you, O God, and how do you want to use me in his or her life? How might I bless him or her?*

Confession: Gently bring before God one or two people who are difficult for you to listen to, maybe even to look at. Confess this inadequacy and pray for God's best for this person. If you're able, ask God to show you how to benefit that person.

Practicing the presence of God: As you talk to people, try praying for them as they speak to you. Even as you mingle in a crowd or shop, pray silently for people (perhaps praying simply, "Peace be with you").

Secrecy: Instead of expressing your opinion about something just because the topic comes up, inquire further about what the other person thinks.

Silence: When someone speaks to you, practice the situational discipline of silencing your mind. As the person speaks, don't think about what you want to reply.

Study: As people speak, study them. Examine how they're standing and what they're doing with their arms. Notice the knit of the eyebrow and the slant of the shoulder. Ask God, *What's going on inside this person that I need to know about? How can I serve this person? How can I be your presence to him or her?*

Submission: When listening to someone, look only at the person instead of looking around or behind the person. Enjoy keeping your gaze intent on the speaker.

Submission: Listen to someone who is not interesting to you and pray for that person.

QUESTIONS FOR DISCUSSION AND REFLECTION

1. What does this chapter lead you to want to pray?
2. What "whole truth" could you talk to Jesus about that might bore other people? (Have fun with this one: model trains, quantum physics, baseball statistics.)
3. Which of these behaviors would you find most difficult if you attempted them?
   - Not looking around as someone speaks to you
   - Keeping your mind quiet and really listening to someone
   - Not expressing your opinion
4. What do such behaviors indicate is probably going on in our hearts?
5. In what situation or to whom do you need to listen better? What would help you do that?

4 Authenticity: True Goodness
and True Realness

Interest in Jesus is intense these days. Movies about Jesus draw people because they see in Jesus a down-to-earth genuineness they may not associate with religion. As my daughter's friend puts it, "Jesus liked all the people my mom said I couldn't hang out with." Even as a little girl, I understood this about Jesus. My father sometimes took me with him to the local bar on Saturdays. On Sundays, my mother took me to church. I somehow knew Jesus would have gone both places. He never thought he was "too good" for anybody—including me.

OUR UNASSUMING SAVIOR

It's ironic to think that the most ethical person who walked the earth did not display moral superiority. He was deeply good but his goodness wasn't off-putting. Instead it was magnetic. It drew people to him. Jesus was free of self-importance and had a way of exposing those who weren't. One of his most frequently quoted phrases was spoken to devout men who routinely pretended to be better than they were: "He who is without sin, let him cast the first stone"

(John 8:7, author's paraphrase).

Picture Jesus at dawn teaching in the temple with people gathered around him (see John 8:2-11). Jesus' opponents drag to him a woman accused of having committed adultery (by herself, it seems), and they make her stand before the group who grasp stones to pelt her with. "Enjoying their sense of moral superiority over her, as well as their sense of having put Jesus in a corner he can't easily escape,"[1] they use her as a tool to trap Jesus in order to accuse him. They clutch their stones, presumably for her but perhaps also to hint to Jesus, "Here's what we do to lawbreakers." The challenge to Jesus was clear: Will you break the law by not condemning her as you have already broken the law by healing people on the Sabbath?

In response to their heated life-and-death challenge, Jesus' response is comical. He squats silently in the sand, making himself lower than the standing woman and vulnerable to anyone's kick or a stray flying stone aimed from behind an accuser's back. What a risk! When they keep demanding an answer, he suggests they just go ahead and stone her — if they have the purity of heart that only God the true judge has. Jesus' reply invites them to show authenticity, to look at themselves and admit who they really are. Are they as good as they pretend to be, or do they have something to hide? He lets that challenge loom in front of them as he turns back to writing in the sand.

You can imagine a modern-day movie audience cheering as each tormentor quietly moves away, leaving the woman alone with Jesus. He has saved her from death; what will she do with her life? By urging her, "Go now and leave your life of sin," he offers her empowerment to live without shame and to pursue truth and genuine love (verse 11). He imparts to her both justice ("If any one of you is without sin") and mercy ("Neither do I condemn you"). Jesus knows that second chances can be transforming, life-giving, and even redemptive. As she abides in his presence for just a few moments, he *loves her into* goodness, drawing her with irresistible grace.

The World God So Loves

People love stories about Jesus and immoral women because they're attracted to the idea of Divine Mercy loving deeply flawed people (see John 4:4-32; Luke 7:36-50;[2] 8:2). I'm intrigued to consider that Jesus ate and drank with those who would rank with today's mobsters (see Matthew 9:10; Luke 5:29; 15:1-2). You have to wonder why those guys put up with a religious prophet and seemed to genuinely like him. Was it because he really listened to them? Because he didn't act as if he were superior? Jesus' "crisp incisive judgments, and the keen satire with which He crumpled up the sophistries of the legal mind . . . appealed to sinners and plain folk, who were sick to death of the eternal wrangling of their religious leaders." This explains why Jesus' disciples included types of people "which never before and never since have felt themselves welcome in religious societies"[3] — a tax collector (which now might be equated with being an extortionist), a political activist, big-business fishermen.

What made Jesus so extraordinarily nonreligious yet deeply good was his insistence on loving the world God so loved while being nothing like it. Christians often get confused about how they should relate to the world — should they separate themselves from it or stay in it and love people? It helps to understand that in the New Testament the word *world* is used at least two different ways. *World* sometimes refers to the whole created order and everyone in it, but other times it refers to "the people who inhabit it, and who have rebelled against their creator, . . . [having] chosen darkness rather than light, and [having] organized itself to oppose the creator."[4] Jesus lived an eternal kind of life *within* the general culture, not separating himself from it. Yet he was nothing like it. He loved people but he didn't act as they did.

Jesus immersed in the world. As a carpenter in his youth and adulthood, Jesus no doubt worked in the huge ongoing construction project of Herod's capital, Sepphoris (four miles from Nazareth), building plazas, theaters, reservoirs, and a palace.[5]

He probably mixed with architects and learned men but also with slaves and day laborers. Because we don't hear of Joseph after the trip to the temple when Jesus was twelve and because Jesus delayed his preaching ministry until he was thirty, seemingly to care for his family, most people conclude that Joseph died while Jesus was still young. If so, Jesus then became a father figure in his family of at least seven siblings or cousins after Joseph died.[6] He would have run the family business and taken leadership roles in his small village. "He knows the difficulty of making ends meet; He knows the difficulty of the ill-mannered customer and the client who will not pay his bills. He knew all the difficulty of living together in an ordinary home and in a big family."[7]

Jesus not of the world. Consider how Jesus must have conducted himself as an independent contractor and small businessman. Any self-employed person knows the temptations to promote oneself, inflate prices, or cut corners when money is tight. With a large family to feed, Jesus must have faced these enticements also. No doubt he did pro-bono work, giving away a table now and then — not a castoff, but a really good one. In certain billing disagreements, he may have let the other guy win. He must have worked hard with great joy without being addicted to his work in order to feel significant.

Perhaps our best clue about Jesus' work style is from his little brother (or cousin) James' description of "wisdom from above." This may describe how James saw Jesus as he conducted business and led the family: "peaceable, gentle, and easy to be intreated, full of mercy and good fruits, without partiality, and without hypocrisy" (James 3:17, KJV). Imagine that with so many kids around, Jesus was *peaceable* among their fights, *gentle* among their roughness, *easy to be entreated* when they needed something, *full of mercy* when they didn't deserve it, *full of good fruits* even when he was sick or it was blazing hot, *without partiality* toward each sibling, and *without hypocrisy* when he truly was better than the rest.

Jesus chose to be the light of the world in the middle of the world—a very different sort of carpenter and itinerant teacher (escaping glory, refusing to be made king, serving his followers in menial ways). Yet he held a compassionate love for the world, noting that the crowds "were harassed and helpless, like sheep without a shepherd" (Matthew 9:36).

Our example. As Jesus prayed for his immediate disciples (and later for all disciples, including us), he asked that God not take us *"out of the world"* but protect us *in* it (John 17:15, italics added). So we are to associate with all types of people in the same profession, workplace, and neighborhood without being influenced by them. Jesus was and is eager to "send out His disciples into [the world], in order to lead the world back to God, and to make the world aware of God."[8]

Those who live an interactive life with God find themselves doing this quite naturally by staying in the world but treating people in other-worldly ways—with love and kindness, by "gentle but firm noncooperation with things that everyone knows to be wrong, together with a sensitive, nonofficious, nonintrusive, nonobsequious service to others."[9] We practice the presence of God in all sorts of situations, praying for those around us, seeking to love whomever stands in front of us at that moment.

Like Jesus, we don't expect the world's approval and we don't strive for it. We understand that "if you belonged to the world, it would love you as its own. . . . That is why the world hates you" (John 15:19). So we differ from the world in *faith* (trusting in Christ, not in wealth or others' opinions), in *purpose* (knowing and loving God, not trying to advance self or live a life of convenience), and in *conduct* (treating people with mercy and justice as we would want to be treated).

NO GAME PLAYING

Jesus' authenticity also showed in how people never had to wonder what he was up to. In conversations and meetings, you may have detected pretense going on and wondered, *What game is this person playing?* You never would have had those thoughts with Jesus. Because he lived in day-to-day interaction with God, who is ultimate reality, Jesus had what 12-step groups call the capacity to "be the same person all the time," what psychology calls an "integrated personality," and what Scripture calls an "undivided heart" (Psalm 86:11). He would be exactly who you thought he was.

Jesus never played games of moral superiority as religious people do who think that because they have found truth, they are somehow better than others. This is pride, which is the central sin from which all others flow, according to the great ones from Augustine[10] to C. S. Lewis.[11] (Lewis called it the "utmost evil.") We need to confess that we pretend to be better than we are, as John Baillie teaches us.[12]

Jesus never pretended. He was the same person off the platform as on the platform. The disciples didn't have to cover up for his bad attitudes or behavior. He taught people to love their neighbors, and then he did it even when those neighbors happened to be an annoyingly persistent blind man or a member of the council who was afraid to be seen with him. Jesus taught people to love their enemies and then forgave his enemies from the cross instead of railing against them. Jesus was not phony, hypocritical, flattering, sanctimonious, counterfeit, deceptive, or misleading. He could be counted on not to scheme or design, connive or manipulate, or change his manner around certain people. Jesus was what we would call "the real deal."

Jesus didn't try to con people into being his followers and justify it by saying it was for the sake of the kingdom of God. He didn't try to recruit followers or get them to donate money to his cause. In fact, he asked followers to weigh carefully if they really wanted what he was offering them. He must have shocked everyone in this setting where some of God's so-called spokespersons postured and positioned themselves in the best light possible.

Simple Directness

Instead of playing games of pretense, Jesus spoke with straightforward candor. He didn't tiptoe around unpleasant facts — what is often described as the elephant sitting in the middle of the room that no one will talk about it. He stated the unspoken intentions of people around him, perhaps leaving them wincing and gulping, such as when he asked, "Why are you trying to kill me?" (John 7:19). These leaders had been privately plotting his death but publicly insisting they were doing no such thing. Many people knew this but wouldn't say anything for "fear of the Jews" (7:13,25). Jesus would have none of their phoniness.

I imagine his followers constantly thought, *I can't believe he said that!* Rarely does anyone talk about the common sin of sexual fantasy or having an "affair of the heart" (see Matthew 5:28). When Jesus did so in the Sermon on the Mount, I'm sure many thought, *How does he know what I did last night?*

Jesus urged his followers not to play religious games but to guard against hypocrisy and to live transparent lives (see Luke 12:1-3). Part of being transparent meant that Jesus did not come off as an unfeeling robot, denying pain, grief, hurt, and abandonment. Authentically human, he openly sobbed several times. He was "deeply moved in spirit and troubled" at Lazarus's tomb and "troubled in spirit" over Judas's betrayal (John 11:33; 13:21). He lived out his Jewish culture of praying laments, expressing on the cross at least the first verse of Psalm 22 and probably the rest of it.

Genuineness

Jesus' unaffected way of living caused him to draw a child next to him — the normal place of highest honor — and say, "Be like this" (see Matthew 18:1-5). This was jarring and difficult in a culture that was not child-centered, as ours is. He wanted his listeners to forget their big ambitions and serve without self-consciousness,[13] doing simple tasks, such as giving cups of cold water earnestly and self-forgetfully.

To interact with Jesus was to know you were loved and not used. To experience Jesus was to experience a deep goodness that left you feeling thankful and reflecting on the greatness of God. To be Jesus' friend was to know he would never abandon you. Jesus didn't use people and even showed mercy to those whom others used (such as the woman caught in adultery). He used *things* and loved *people*, while our current society advocates acquiring things but objectifying people as consumers, potential customers (or church members), and "useful" contacts.

AUTHENTICALLY GOOD?

The idea that some people are "too good to be true" has caused us to compromise authenticity so that it lacks the genuine purity of the way Jesus lived it. He managed to be deeply good but also down-to-earth — never putting himself above others. If we can't imagine authenticity combined with goodness, we may elevate authenticity and demote the goodness that is the fruit of the Spirit. Here are two ways this happens.

Being proud of being bad. In an effort to relate to people and to have nothing to do with phoniness, Christians may go out of their way to prove they aren't overly religious through choice of language, clothing, and social habits. The issue isn't so much the actions themselves but all the effort put into being *real*. This is a reaction, I believe, to having seen other Christians display moral superiority, if not in words and deeds, then in an inner attitude that leaks into tone of voice and unspoken inferences. To refrain from this hypocrisy, it may seem expedient to strive to show how average we are, as if to say, "I'm as bad as the rest of you" or "You think that's bad? Here's what I did!" But this switches the focus from Christ and his power to transform us to me and my flaws.

This effort is often combined with an emphasis on grace that translates into the thought, *You're accepted no matter what, so don't concern yourself that you're not Mother Teresa.* Scripture's emphasis on grace as empowerment is not mentioned, nor is our gradual transformation into Christlikeness, because that makes us seem less than *real.*

But Jesus didn't equate authenticity with the glory of being average. He didn't eliminate from life the power of God to change us and the majesty of God to draw us into the kingdom life. He urged us to long for a growing purity of heart and to spur one another on to such things. The deep goodness and beauty of Jesus and how the Holy Spirit works in us do not need to be forfeited for the sake of being relevant.

I confess that when I first began speaking to groups, I relished being told that I was "real." I was reacting to speakers who made the Christian life seem simplistically formulaic and others who perhaps unintentionally gave the impression they had "arrived." But as I desired to live in the kingdom of God, that emphasis on being real faded. God and God's kingdom became more important than how I was perceived.

Showcasing woundedness. Another well-intentioned effort toward authenticity is to focus primarily on brokenness. This happens because churches and families have sometimes denied woundedness and hurts in an attempt to become good, faithful, hopeful Christians. But since the wounds go unaddressed, the brokenness gets covered up with legalism. When those of us working through brokenness from the past find freedom from condemnation and rejection in honest community with others, we may state out loud unattractive facts and feelings that have been denied. Some Christians thank us for our honesty, and others wish we'd get over it and just be positive.

While it is crucial to be forthright in certain ways about the hurts of our past and present, we can become unable to see that there is more. I confess this was me also. I found such healing in being able to confess truth about my faults and hurts and find grace from God that these things became my life themes, so to speak. As I began to understand life in the kingdom of God and embrace hope, I was worried that it would force me back into denial, numbness, and pretense.

Two ideas helped. First, I saw that the Old Testament prophets offered not only truth (no matter how painful it may be) but also hope (no matter how far-fetched it may seem),[14] while I embraced truth but not hope. Woundedness had become my identity — the biggest thing about me — rather than Jesus.

Second, I saw that although Jesus treated the wounded with great tenderness (see Matthew 12:20), he always pointed people to the way forward. He never minimized pain and heartache, careful to avoid scolding the shattered, half-doubting father of the demon-possessed boy who said, "I do believe; help me overcome my unbelief!" (Mark 9:24). Like that father, I believed such a life was possible but I also did not fully trust God enough. I was so relieved that Jesus accepted the father's brutal honesty and then met his needs by healing his son. Jesus listened deeply to people's troubles, wept over them, and never told people to "get over it"; but he did invite them to enlarge their faith and take whatever their next step might be in trusting God.

Jesus managed to be down-to-earth and exceptionally real but also hopeful. He spoke difficult truths that others overlooked but still offered hope that living an eternal kind of life is possible here and now; traveling the journey of transformation toward Christlikeness is realistic; connecting with God can not only change us but bring oneness with God. To embrace hope does not mean that we stop telling the truth or that we minimize it. In fact, it means telling more of the truth. Jesus embraced both truth-telling and hope of life in the kingdom. Gradually I did too.

JESUS, THE "REAL DEAL"

Part of the reason these versions of authenticity appeal to us is that Jesus' ability to be deeply good *and* deeply real is foreign to us. We haven't experienced many people who are truly good without being goody-goody, and so we don't know how to do that.

It helps to focus on how Jesus' goodness was not offensive but attractive, even magnetic. Jesus' rightness exceeded that of the scribes and Pharisees (see Matthew 5:20) because his deep goodness flowed from who he was. Those mobsters liked him (even though he was good) because what he said rang true like nothing else they'd ever heard. He was clearly in touch with the realities of the universe and they knew it. When he taught, even in conversation, hearts *burned* (see Luke 24:32). I confess that sometimes Jesus' goodness has frustrated me because I have thought, *I'll never be that good.* I'm learning that my spirituality is not about me, however, but about Jesus and connecting with Jesus in the next ten minutes. So I allow myself to be drawn to him as the disciples were who made these intense exclamations:

- "'Even if I have to die with you, I will never disown you.' And all the others said the same" (Mark 14:31).
- "Lord, I am ready to go with you to prison and to death" (Luke 22:33).
- "I will lay down my life for you" (John 13:37).

These statements were not just emotional outbursts. These disciples eventually did lay down their lives for Jesus. They had never seen anyone like him — nor have we.

EXPERIMENTS IN CONNECTING WITH GOD
(Spiritual Practices to Consider)

To RECEIVE this authenticity from God

Meditation: Read John 8:1-11 and picture it happening. Who does God invite you to be — one of the religious leaders or the woman or a disciple standing by? Write down the feelings you would have had if you had been that person. What do you most admire about Jesus in this passage?

Study. Read what wise Christians have written about pride and humility (*Humility* by Andrew Murray; "The Great Sin," chapter 8 of book 3 of *Mere Christianity* by C. S. Lewis[15]). Then write a prayer and respond to God about this.

Worship: Recount to Jesus the things about him that amaze you most.

To BECOME one who offers the authenticity of Jesus to others

Confession: Ask God to show you when you are pretending to be better than you are. Then find a friend on the same path and meet to confess this. Be prepared to laugh and impart grace to each other.

Listening prayer: Ask God to show you where you are giving in to phoniness or demeaning attempts to be real.

Reflection: Journal about these questions: How might God be asking you to be not *of* the world? Is that request in line with your will and your true desires? (Be honest.) Do you need to confess that you want the world's approval and ask God to help you? If so, what part of the world has a hold on you (e.g., pleasing others, looking good, receiving praise, getting what you want)? If so, don't despair. It takes time. We'll revisit the process in chapter 14 on dying to self.

Service: How might God be leading you into the world — perhaps to volunteer in a community organization or a professional group? Or join a community-oriented hobby or sports group?

QUESTIONS FOR DISCUSSION AND REFLECTION

1. What impresses you most about Jesus in the scene with the woman caught in adultery?
2. In what ways are Christians today a lot like the world, especially character-wise?
3. Which of the following elements of Jesus' authenticity are you most drawn to? Why?
   - Lacking moral superiority
   - In the world but not of the world
   - Directness
   - Genuineness — no pretense
   - Having a deep goodness that was infectious
   - Other
4. What does this chapter lead you to want to pray?
5. Which of the listed experiments do you see yourself trying out this week?

5   Welcoming the Stranger

I liked the idea better when it was only talked about in the leadership meeting. Putting it into action was difficult. The idea, the "three-minute guideline," suggested that in the last three minutes before the church service began and in the first three minutes afterward, leaders would greet only people we didn't know. While I've always felt empathetic toward newcomers, I found I really just wanted to talk to the people I knew. It was . . . easier, more fun.

When I tried talking to newcomers, I couldn't think of what to say. So I made a little "cheat sheet" of welcoming and informative things to say (parking issues, location of Sunday school or bathrooms) and tucked it in my Bible. Week after week, I took a deep breath and launched out to greet unsuspecting newcomers. It turned out to be delightful to give them this bit of love, and I learned so much. I saw that many people were nervous and longed to have someone talk to them. I realized that I had been cocooning safely in my own space and needed to reach out to others.

Such is the spiritual practice of welcoming the stranger, a common practice for those living in the kingdom of God. Not often listed as a spiritual discipline, it's a practice Jesus emphasized by how he welcomed all kinds of people into his life and identified with them:

"When I was a stranger, you welcomed me" (Matthew 25:35, CEV) ". . . when you did it for the least of these, you did it for me" (verse 40, author's paraphrase). Such welcoming is tangible and helpful, even offering them a cup of cold water (see Matthew 10:40-42; see also Matthew 18:5; John 13:20).

To welcome strangers means cultivating an invitational spirit and offering a sense of "home" to others (see John 14:23). We pay attention to others, inviting them to be at home with us as they unfold themselves before us (as God invites us to do). We wait for them to be able to do that. "To merely welcome another, to provide for them, to make a place, is one of the most life-giving and life-receiving things a human being can do."[1]

Some call this practice hospitality, but hospitality has become limited to inviting others to eat with us or stay in our home. While cleaning, bed making, and food preparation are valuable gifts to offer others, the core idea is that of being open and vulnerable to a person's needs.

Additionally, welcoming the stranger takes the focus away from just having friends over to reaching out to people who for some reason are considered strangers. You see this in Jesus' way of welcoming people whom others routinely ignored: beggars, hobbling lepers, demon-possessed people. Jesus grouped this practice of welcoming strangers with helping others who are often overlooked: the hungry, the thirsty, the naked, the sick, and the imprisoned (see Matthew 25:35-36). In the "graduate sermon" he preached upon returning as a teacher to his hometown of Nazareth, Jesus marked out his purpose to minister to such people: to bring good news to the poor, freedom to prisoners, recovery of sight for the blind; to release the oppressed; to proclaim the year of the Lord's favor (see Luke 4:18-19).

Even though this sermon nearly got him killed for highlighting how two Gentiles (strangers!) welcomed a prophet, Jesus was merely emphasizing the tender commands of the law (the widow of Zarephath and the Syrian Naaman; see Luke 4:25-27). Because the Israelites had been sojourners (immigrants) in Egypt, God laid it down that strangers were to be protected by the same laws that governed Israel (see Deuteronomy 1:16; 24:17; 27:19). Furthermore, Israelites were to go above and beyond decent behavior and *love* strangers (see Deuteronomy 10:19, NRSV). In the Sermon on the Mount when Jesus taught about going the extra mile, he applied it to a Roman soldier — clearly an uncomfortable stranger for the Jews (see Matthew 5:41). In God's kingdom, God knows no strangers, and so he invites us to live such a life here and now.

WHEN THE STRANGER DOES THE WELCOMING

Jesus illustrated this welcoming spirit by inventing a story in which someone normally viewed as a stranger goes the extra mile and becomes the one who welcomes. In a culture in which the only good Samaritan was a dead Samaritan, Jesus created a "stranger" — a Samaritan who resembled himself. Try to be one of Jesus' listeners to this story and imagine the shock and perhaps revulsion you might have felt (see Luke 10:25-37).

First, the road from Jerusalem to Jericho is steep and scary — perhaps a robbery has occurred there the day before Jesus tells this story. The priest and the Levite who do not stop to help the injured man are simply doing the sensible, no-brainer thing. They watch out for themselves; what if the robber is hanging around and plans to attack them?

Jesus portrayed the one we call the Good Samaritan as being full of empathy. (I picture him as actor Morgan Freeman.) He helps the beaten man, not concerning himself that a Jew wouldn't want our hero touching him. The Samaritan easily puts himself in another person's shoes because thinking and feeling with others is part of who he is. He also seems to be the kind of person who helps people automatically. He doesn't have to think, *I'd better do a good deed today.* It isn't a duty — he's not part of the Jerusalem-to-Jericho Road

Safety Program. If you drop a piece of paper, he automatically stoops to pick it up. Then he winks at you and goes on. Helping is no big deal to him.

While we may limit our service to designated serving roles (such as serving as a priest or a Levite), the Samaritan serves without a special role. All three *see* the wounded man, but only the Samaritan has *compassion*. He serves without self-consciousness, title, or position. Serving is part of how he lives and breathes.

Also, this Samaritan is not chintzy in his service. He gives the innkeeper more than needed and doesn't ask the innkeeper to give him a better rate because it's for a good cause. Best of all, the Samaritan is relational. He takes care of the man himself and so probably gets dirty and has to delay or cancel his business.

We have to wonder how the injured Jew feels when he wakes up at the inn. Is he horrified that a Samaritan has touched him? Would he have preferred to die rather than be tended to by a Samaritan?

Jesus challenges us to regard how God has welcomed us and to welcome others with God's love. To do that we have to let go of self-absorption so we can pay attention to others — and let go of being indifferent to people we don't know or who are not in our group. Jesus invites us to ask ourselves, *Whom do I regard as a Samaritan?*

Today the Samaritan might be a sex offender. A few years ago, my friend asked me to look at a website that listed sex offenders in our area because her son had been convicted of Internet child pornography and she wondered if he was listed there. I didn't find her son, but the first name and picture on the list was my favorite client at the Samaritan Center (a drop-in center for the homeless). I'll call him Nick. I particularly liked him because he was always polite, saying thank you for whatever I did. He kept his clothes neat, so I had wondered why he kept getting fired from every job when he was obviously such a hard worker. I had even offered to recommend him to someone I knew who needed a good tenant, but he didn't take me up on the offer. Nor did he accept my invitation to join our family for a holiday meal.

To see Nick's picture on that website horrified me. I had been welcoming this stranger for many months, not knowing his offense. What would I do now? I prayed that I would surrender the situation to God.

When my weekly volunteering day came around, I told the director about this, and she was surprised — yet she wasn't. "That must be why he comes in here black and blue on most Mondays," she reminded me. "On the weekend, people find him and beat him up." When Nick arrived I found I was ready to greet him as always. What did not go so well was washing his clothes. I began sobbing as I did so. What had happened to Nick as a child for him to respond this way? We eventually learned that his offense had occurred twenty years before and he had never repeated it. Being pictured on the website meant he couldn't keep a job and that he would be beaten up regularly. This was his life.

For years I had easily welcomed all our clients — some of whom have been in jail for drug-related offenses — but with Nick I hesitated. I was able to do it only by picturing how Jesus would have done it. That connecting moment with God allowed me to abide in Jesus and Jesus to abide in me. In previous months, I had been praying that God would give me a heart of greater compassion, to let everything in me that rejects people flow out of me. Praying for Nick and serving him was clearly part of my soul school.

WHO ARE OUR STRANGERS?

People appear to us as strangers for different reasons, but they usually fit into one of these categories:

Outcasts. A person's past didn't disqualify him or her from Jesus' welcome. While most rabbis threw stones at lepers, Jesus welcomed them (see Matthew 8:1-4; Mark 1:40-45; Luke 5:12-15; 17:11-19). He touched these untouchables.

Wrongdoers. As for wrongdoers, Jesus not only greeted Zacchaeus (a tax collector) in his hidden spot in the tree but also made him the host, inviting himself to be Zacchaeus's dinner guest (see Luke 19:1-10). The immoral past of the Samaritan woman did not disqualify her either. In fact, Jesus went out of his way to extend himself: "He *had* to go through Samaria" (John 4:4, italics added). He welcomed this person, who was also a stranger ethnically and gender-wise. He should not have had a conversation with a woman in public, but he not only did so, he also invited her to enter into a deepened relationship with God.

People longing for home. At one time Joseph, Mary, and Jesus were strangers as political refugees, having to leave their homeland, the sacred space of God's chosen people. Imagine their fear as they slipped out of Bethlehem by night and made a two- to three-week journey on a route frequented by robbers (especially in light of their three treasures, some of which they may have used to pay their way). This Jewish couple mixed with non-Jews, having to trust God every step of the way. They were also grieving, weeping over the slaughter of the innocent babies (see Matthew 2:13-18).

As political refugees, they needed to make a life in Egypt for possibly two years. Some benevolent Egyptian must have hired Joseph as a carpenter, even though he was a Jew. Did Egyptian women befriend Mary? Any kindness they were shown would have influenced how Mary heard the positive references to Gentiles in Jesus' "graduate sermon" (see Luke 4:18-19). Unlike the other listeners, she had rubbed shoulders with Gentiles and probably received their kindness. They weren't strangers to her.

Anyone who isn't like me. When we see or meet people who differ from us politically, ethnically, or theologically, a little "ping" may go off in our head that says, *Ooh, different. Step back.* Ponder what Jesus' disciple Simon the Zealot thought when Jesus healed and then praised the faith of a Roman centurion. Simon would have viewed the centurion as a prime candidate for assassination and "fuel for the fires of hell."[2] As we draw circles of who's in and who's out, we make strangers of those who worship Christ from another corner of the kingdom.

A stranger may just be someone of a different economic class. In a church full of homeowners, an apartment dweller often feels like a stranger. A disabled person is a stranger in the midst of fitness buffs as is a nonreader among well-read folks. Military kids or missionary kids, parolees or drug rehab graduates may all qualify as strangers among those without that experience.

Newcomers to any situation exist as strangers because they don't know what's going on, while others do. That's why we want to provide maps to people's homes when a church activity occurs there. People have told me about wanting to come to a church activity in a home but getting lost. During announcements, it was said, "Everybody knows where X lives," but they didn't. In our times of connecting with God, God helps us think about these issues and become eager to welcome all.

Anyone we're tempted to exclude and ignore. Strangers are often people in power-down positions: "children as opposed to adults, women as opposed to men, minority races as opposed to majority races, the poor as opposed to middle-class, the middle-class as opposed to rich, lower-paid workers as opposed to highly paid workers, less educated as opposed to more educated, blue-collar workers as opposed to professionals."[3] The elderly are easily overlooked. When my quiet, eighty-year-old mother-in-law came to visit, our other dinner guests never engaged her in conversation. I wept later to think of the many times I had neglected to speak to an older person.

If we're honest, we want to push away some people because of their personality. C. S. Lewis cited the boring person: "It's so much easier to *pray* for a bore than to *go and see* him."[4] Or we may avoid pushy people, people who talk too long about themselves, those who scream and pout for what they feel they deserve, know-it-alls, or people who let their kids run wild. In any "us versus them" situation, "them" are the strangers.

The shocking thing about Jesus is that he did not merely tolerate such different people. Jesus offered himself to them in self-giving love.

The Least of These

Related to the discipline of welcoming the stranger is *associating with the lowly*. While describing love, Paul wrote, "Live in harmony with one another; do not be haughty, but *associate with the lowly*; do not claim to be wiser than you are" (Romans 12:16, NRSV, italics added). *The Message* puts it, "Get along with each other; don't be stuck-up. *Make friends with nobodies*; don't be the great somebody" (italics added). Jesus went out of his way to mix with people we might avoid — crossing the Sea of Galilee to the region of the Gerasenes to heal the demon-possessed man, refusing to ignore the shouting, insistent Bartimaeus but turning to him and saying, "What do you want me to do for you?" (see Mark 5:1-20; 10:46-52).

Associating with the lowly means making friends of those normally overlooked and those not normally sought out. To befriend such a one transforms us. It keeps us from pretending to be wiser than we are because "those we are caring for become our teachers. Personal contact with persons who are disadvantaged in some way can be a powerful means of transformation for Jesus' apprentices."[5] So this practice is not only about *helping* those deemed lowly, but forming a reciprocal relationship with them so that we *learn* from them and from Jesus how to not be haughty or think we're wiser than we are.

The lowly are the needy for whom God is a guardian (see Psalm 12:5). God gives mercy to the poor and urges us to create a sense of home as "a father to the fatherless" and "a defender of widows" (Psalm 68:5). To oppress the poor (such as passing laws that prohibit "camping" within city limits when sleeping under a bridge or bush is one's only option) is to show "contempt for their Maker," but to be "kind to the needy honors God" (Proverbs 14:31). Instead God insists on justice for these persons: "Defend the cause of the weak and fatherless; maintain the rights of the poor and oppressed" (Psalm 82:3).

Jesus' example of welcoming these lowly strangers tells us that donating money is good, but not enough. Always relational, Jesus looked people in the face, sat down with them, ate with them, and listened to them without running over them. He understood reciprocity in relationships, asking the outcast Samaritan woman for a drink of water. As we abide in Christ, we are enabled to welcome such strangers by opening ourselves and being willing to be helped by these persons today.

FROM HOSTILITY TO HOSPITALITY

Welcoming the stranger may require that we examine what holds us back and ask God to help us explore why particular people make us uncomfortable. It could be old prejudices, or perhaps we're just shy. The latter was my dilemma with the three-minute guideline. But in trying it out, I rediscovered a truth I already knew: Newcomers were relieved that I spoke first because they were shy also. By practicing the presence of God in the midst of it—asking God, *What do I need to know to reach out to this person?*—I overcame the shyness and things flowed naturally (and even supernaturally).

Jesus' way of welcoming strangers shows his deep empathy with others. He sought to know how people felt, and he thought about how he could be helpful. The practice of welcoming strangers schools us in this empathy as we "look not only to [our] own interests, but also to the interests of others" (Philippians 2:4). It helps us learn to care more about how the other feels than how I look (should I talk to my neighbor if I'm wearing torn pants or my hair is wet?) or how my home looks (should I ask that person to step inside if my home is not neat and clean?). Meeting people's needs becomes more important.

You hear a voice inside you asking, *Am I trying to impress people or love them?* As a result, we gradually become unself-conscious, easy, and automatic in loving the people we encounter every day.

LIVING FROM THE HEART?

At this point, you may be wondering if it's phony to try a practice such as the three-minute guideline if you're not eager to welcome strangers. Shouldn't people get their hearts right before trying such a thing (or other practices suggested at the end of each chapter in this book)?

This question points to how spiritual formation works. It's about connecting with God in a soul-friend relationship, which helps us (1) live from an increasingly right heart (or spirit) and (2) let everything we *do* flow from that. So if we *want* to welcome strangers better, we need to cultivate a welcoming heart. That's why it's important to look at what might be holding us back. Many of the practices at the end of each chapter (especially the first section about receiving, absorbing, or experiencing Jesus' qualities) help us cultivate a right heart by connecting with God in some way.

As we're led, however, we try out practices also. While we're in the process of cultivating that right heart, we use practices to prayerfully retrain the body to *do* these things, because even with a right heart, the body (and its automatic responses) will not follow suit without some nudging. So we connect with God, follow God's leading about practices, and try out a few — without being a martyr! To try practices that are *far beyond* my reach would be phony; to try practices *a little beyond* my reach is to trust God. (Although now and then, God leads us to leap. But this is unusual, not typical.) So as we get our heart right, we ask God to show us what outward practices would move us forward through soul school.

Besides, outward actions can produce inward change. An outward practice (about which I'm willing but hesitant) connects me with God so that I develop a right heart by *doing* that outward practice. Practicing the three-minute guideline helped me rely on God, which increased my desire to welcome strangers. This isn't faking it but letting God work in me in a practical way. It's about "trying on" life in the kingdom of God as I get used to it.

EXPERIMENTS IN CONNECTING WITH GOD
(Spiritual Practices to Consider)

To RECEIVE God's welcome to you

Meditation: Read Luke 10:25-37 and picture it happening. Write down the feelings you would have had if you had been the innkeeper or the beaten person or even the Samaritan.

Meditation: First, consider who is the last person you'd want to see on the side of the road needing your help. Picture Jesus helping that individual. Feast on Jesus' heart of compassion. As you're ready, see yourself beside Jesus helping the person.

Prayer: Consider the times you have been a stranger. Thank God for the people who welcomed you.

To BECOME one who offers such welcoming to strangers

Fellowship and reflection: Ask a friend to help you identify the strangers in your life. Don't balk at odd ideas your friend may bring up. Pray that God will then show you how to welcome certain strangers a little more.

Intercessory prayer: Look through your newspaper for stories about anyone who is a "stranger" to you, especially immigrants, the disabled, or people who are in trouble with the law. Read the article with an effort to understand their world. Pray for these persons' wholeness in Christ, and pray for your increased capacity to welcome them in your life.

Practicing the presence of God: Greet a newcomer at work, in your neighborhood, or at church, asking God to show you this person's needs.

Welcoming the stranger: Look into the eyes of the next homeless person you pass and smile at him or her. (Most folks don't look into their eyes, even if they give them money.)

Welcoming the stranger: Choose someone who is a stranger to you in some way. Pray for that person and then ask God to show you how to engage him or her in a conversation, beginning with a warm greeting and a question.

QUESTIONS FOR DISCUSSION AND REFLECTION

1. What resonated most with you about the story of the Good Samaritan?
2. Who are the strangers in your life?
3. How does it help us to "associate with the lowly"?
4. How might you welcome strangers on a personal level?
5. How might you welcome strangers at the church level?

PART 2

JESUS, THE PROACTIVE LOVER

6 Compassion That Flows

While I have to push myself to do something compassionate — make dinner for an ailing friend or give away frequent flyer miles — compassion flowed out of Jesus as naturally as water runs downhill. It was a deeply rooted part of who he was.

In fact, it looks as though Jesus couldn't help himself. He was so moved with compassion that he dared to interrupt — actually, disrupt — a funeral procession (see Luke 7:11-17, especially verse 13, NRSV). While many of Jesus' healings involved people asking for help for themselves or for a friend or family member, this time he barged in without being asked. Why would he do that?

Picture Jesus walking into the small Galilean town of Nain. As he and his crowd of followers approach the town gate, they see a corpse being carried out — "the only son of his mother, and she was a widow" (verse 12). Her predicament of having no male next of kin left her at the mercy of her relatives — would they take her in (and perhaps treat her like a servant)? If not, how would she survive? Begging? Prostitution?

"Moved with compassion," no doubt by her dilemma, Jesus immediately tells her, "Don't cry." Then he turns to the dead young man, touches the basketlike coffin, and talks to him! This strikes me as the oddest thing Jesus ever did. Have you ever seen someone talk to a corpse? Perhaps only in movies.

What's even odder is that the dead man sits up and talks to Jesus. We don't know what they say to each other or what the mother says when Jesus scoops up the young man out of his basket-coffin and hands him to his mother. Others' responses are recorded: They are filled with awe and praise God; "A great prophet has appeared among us," they said. "God has come to help his people" (verse 16). Shortly before this, four miles away in Jesus' hometown of Nazareth, the townspeople had attempted to throw him off a cliff. What do they say on this day when they hear about what Jesus has done in Nain? Are they jealous because he didn't do this miracle in Nazareth?

Since compassion doesn't stream from most of us as naturally as it did from Jesus, we need regular spiritual practices to learn how to have compassion and show compassion. That's why I need to show up every week to volunteer at the Samaritan Center. I need to *practice* compassion in order to have it flow from me.

Sometimes practices grow out of situations we're already in but disgruntled about. For example, a few years ago I found myself weary of air travel. Even though I occupied myself at the gate and on the plane by working on my laptop, I disliked sitting hip to hip with strangers in the plane. All the grumbling and competing to be first in any line (especially as we wait to deplane) tempted the unconverted parts of my soul to be crabby. I particularly didn't like waiting at the gate because of what is called "people watching" — people observing each other with no thought of how God views them or wants to use us in their lives. If you look up, people even look away so as to avoid any personal interaction. This activity reinforces the idea that we *use* others as objects for diversion or even entertainment instead of regarding them as people God asks us to love and show compassion to.

My attitude deteriorated to the point of grouchiness, so I asked God to help me come up with a spiritual practice for when I fly. I thought of it as I watched what happens when someone drops something in an airport. Most people stare; others snicker. Why couldn't I jump up and help?

So I recast my reasons for going to the airport this way: Ten or fifteen times a year I go to the airport to help people (not merely to fly), especially older people. If I see someone drop something, I pick it up. If people struggle to get their luggage into an overhead bin, I jump up and help them. If a child looks lost (or leaves behind a stuffed animal — very common), I help the child. If someone looks upset, I pray for him or her and ask God for guidance about whether I should speak to the person. These are now my primary reasons for going to the airport, but since I'm there, I catch my scheduled flight. Quickly I added an element of near-secrecy by not waiting to be thanked. I'm the "airport pixie" — appearing when you need me and disappearing otherwise.

This silly-sounding practice has taken away my grouchiness, but it is also teaching me to act immediately on my pathetically small nudges of compassion. If I sense people don't want help, I back off. But I no longer stand there and think, *Should I or shouldn't I help this person?*

Jesus' life shows us that unself-consciously helping someone who stumbles or picking up what someone drops or automatically grinning at the weary person who is people-watching us comes from deep within. Such transformation of life is possible even for a self-absorbed person like me growing up as the baby of my family. I am not hopeless — I need only connect with Jesus and let his compassion pour forth.

SYMPATHY OF THE SOUL

Jesus was so permeated with love that it's as if he was made of a different substance. Often Jesus' miracles are spoken about as if they were only displays of power to prove his divinity. While they certainly functioned as signs of God's love, power, and glory breaking into a searching, confused world, the gospel writers went out of their way to emphasize how these miracles flowed from his compassion (see Matthew 9:36; 20:29-34; Mark 1:39-41; 5:19, KJV; 6:34; Luke 7:11-16). He did them because he loved people.

For Jesus there was no such thing as being harsh, hardhearted, remote, cold, distant, callous, or without pity. He would walk across the sea to come and help you. Normally he traveled by land or in a boat like the rest of us, but that one time the disciples needed him out there, he showed up. Jesus does very odd things, if necessary, to come to us and meet our needs. We should expect to be shocked.

In the healings of demon-possessed people, his compassion proved greater than fear or disgust. While we would be alarmed by meeting terrorists or seriously disturbed mental patients who have escaped (evoking a similar response from us that New Testament demoniacs would have had from those around them), Jesus' compassion overrode his realistic knowledge of evil and demonic power.

Out of compassion, Jesus warned his disciples about his upcoming death so they'd not be so devastated. After the feedings of the crowds, he gathered up the fragments — was this because he had a particular need in mind? To give them to his favorite first-century soup kitchen? To help the boy's mother, who may have sent him to sell the loaves and fish to bring home much-needed income? As a way of life, Jesus could not pass up comforting the distressed, and he refused to be inattentive to the hardships of others.

I'm most impressed that Jesus responded so well to interruptions, which most of his miracles were. In each case, he had somewhere to go and something to do, but he delayed these things because a needy person stood in front of him. When asked for help by a man who was living death — covered with leprous sores, a mass of mangled flesh and tendons (see Matthew 8:1-4; Luke 5:12-16) — he made a point of choosing to stop and heal and to say, "I am willing." He readily gave to those who had no prior claim on him.

Likewise, Jesus did not cut corners in healing (as I would have) but "went throughout Galilee . . . healing *every* disease and sickness among the people. News about him spread all over Syria, and people brought to him all who were ill with various diseases, those suffering severe pain, the demon-possessed, those having seizures, and the paralyzed, and he healed them" (Matthew 4:23-24, italics added). Jesus constantly heard the cries of people's souls: "When he saw the crowds, he had compassion on them, because they were harassed and helpless, like sheep without a shepherd" (Matthew 9:36).

Tears of Jesus

The life of Jesus shows us the struggle of God as well as the serenity of God. We find the Anointed One in tears several times, once at the tomb of his dead friend Lazarus (see John 11:35), where he shuddered and his whole frame shook with grief.[1] Many people point to this as proof that he was a real human being, not a divine being pretending to be human. While it may do that, it is even more a picture of our compassionate God, who sobs. "The Word, through whom the worlds were made, weeps like a baby at the grave of his friend."[2] If you view God as a dry-eyed being, do as Jesus told us — forget what you think you know about the nature of God and lose yourself in him as a picture of our Father (see Matthew 11:25-27; John 3:13; 17:6-8).

Jesus as a weeping Savior mirrors God, who, in grief, drenches the nations with tears. God's heart throbs like a harp (see Isaiah 16:9,11; 21:3; 22:4; 25:8; see also Genesis 6:6; Psalm 78:40; Isaiah 63:10). A frequent cry of God throughout the prophets is "Return to me,"[3] because our grieving God wants us back when we stray. Poet Gerard Manley Hopkins pictured this for us: "The Holy Ghost over the bent World *broods*."[4] When people "just don't get it" and miss who God is and what God invites us to (as both Israel and the mourners at Lazarus's tomb did), the Trinity takes to weeping.

Jesus wept even for his enemies. In the scene in which Jesus wept over Jerusalem (see Luke 19:40-44), the verb for "weeping" there indicates "walking and sobbing. He speaks in a broken sentence, which suggests powerful emotion,"[5] lamenting, "If only you had known what would bring you peace . . ." (Luke 19:42, author's paraphrase). "Jesus' tears are at the core of the Christian gospel. This was not a moment of regrettable weakness, something a real Messiah ought to have avoided."[6]

Nor were these tears of bitterness, but rather of grief that Jerusalem, the center of religious life that didn't recognize God come-in-the-flesh, would soon be destroyed by the Roman army. In spite of his repeated warnings to Jerusalem, Jesus didn't gloat at their doom.

> There is no sense of "I told you so" or "It serves you
> right"; only the shaking sobs of the prophet like
> Jeremiah. . . . The terrible judgment . . . proceeds
> not from a stern and cold justice but a heart of love,
> that wants the best for, and from, the people, and
> so must now oppose, with sorrow and tears, the
> rebellion that had set its own interests and agendas
> before those of God. . . . Those tears are not just the
> human reaction to a sad and frustrating situation.
> They are the tears of the God of love.[7]

Compassion: Prayer and Action

Jesus' tears encompassed feelings but also action. His compassionate life moved in a significant rhythm of an inward life of prayer and an outward life of action. He was a person of "both prayer and action, who could be continually mindful of God and yet be fully present with people as an attentive empathetic healer."[8] He prayed constantly — not just when casting out demons, healing incurable diseases, or feeding crowds but also during his baptism and the Transfiguration (see Luke 3:21; 9:29). He often withdrew to lonely places, spending the night praying (see 5:16; 6:12).

This undermines the often-stated idea of the Mary-Martha split — that a person is either a pray-er or a doer. Prayer and activity blend together because as we pray for others, we're moved by their predicament and answer a nudge to move into action. In the midst of action, we become overwhelmed by others' needs and our inadequacies, so we are driven to prayer to meet these needs. Even as we serve, we practice the presence of God, praying as our hands move to help.

This active response of compassion should not be underestimated. Many of us lament that we don't have deeper feelings of compassion for people, but what is important is to be learning to respond to each nudge of compassion from God with merciful *action*. Our goal is to become continually more alert to these prods to action from God rather than waiting until we have certain feelings about people.

Weeping Prayer as a Discipline

While many people say, "I cry only at movies" (even men), Jesus cried over real people and real events. Like him, we must not be hardened to the happenings of the world God so loves: people suffering with AIDS, children trapped in sex trafficking, victims of worldwide hurricanes and earthquakes. These are all real people whom God deeply loves. We're called to join God in weeping for them, in letting our "heart be broken by the things that break the heart of God"[9] regularly.

Instances occur daily that cause God to weep, and it's good for our souls to join God in such weeping because it connects us with God in a deeper way as we search out and know the mind of God. And of course, it builds the compassionate "mind of Christ" in us (1 Corinthians 2:12,16).

Alertness and awareness. To avoid slipping into complacency, we need to make ourselves aware of tragedy on a regular basis. For me this involves reading the world news section of the newspaper daily to see what is happening that would cause God to weep. Where are the poor, the needy, and the oppressed suffering today? What new or continuing guerrilla warfare or natural disaster has caused people just like me to become widowed or orphaned? Who has been lied to and defrauded? Who has been left without a home? How are the hurts of the past being mended — or not? What is happening today in yesterday's crisis locations: Rwanda? Kosovo? Vietnam? Being present and attentive to those in crisis is part of how we colabor with God as a light in the darkness.

Being acquainted with the news may not be enough to adequately inform us of what the people whom God longs for are experiencing. We need to walk among suffering folks. After I spoke at a conference in Guatemala, a relative asked me what sights I saw. I began with what affected me most — visiting the Guatemala City dump. The day before my visit, eight children had slipped down through the garbage and suffocated underneath it.

"Why in the world did you go to such a place?" he howled.

I wasn't sure what to say. "Because I needed to?"

At the time, I didn't have words to explain, so I went on to describe how I got to walk behind the missionary nurse who works there. Those living in the shanties on the fringe of the dump greeted her with hugs. The pregnant women caught her eye and grinned, as did those whose injuries she had bandaged the day before. Children cozied up to her, knowing that bits of candy would soon slip out of her pocket and into their hands. Back at her clinic in the midst of the lean-tos, we fed children, and I watched her do her medical wonders. I felt as if I had walked behind Jesus all afternoon.

Later, I knew why I had requested to visit the dump. I was becoming too complacent in my daily life and needed to be immersed in how the rest of the world lives. While volunteering at a drop-in center for the homeless has meant a great deal to me, our facility would be like Club Med in Guatemala. It had been too long since I'd been out of the United States, and I needed to see an impoverished child of God sitting right in front of me once again and know this was *normal* in that place. I needed to weep and make compassionate decisions

in the day when I call.
This I know, that God is for me.

third reading of the passage (Psalm 56:1-9, NRSV), I found
ing out, "When she is afraid, help her put her trust in you.
ink, O God, 'This I know, that God is for me!' Help her be
and declare, 'What can flesh do to me?' Make her ene-
t in the day when I call.'" I also prayed, I confess, *Repay*
ir crime. In such prayers, we keep company with God in
room of *chronos* time, crying over the tragic news of the
not choose to stand in the light of God's life.

ing this compassion of Jesus can be draining unless we
ve in the light of God's compassion for us. We can love
he first loves us (see 1 John 4:19). So part of our con-
God includes receiving such compassion from God,
ow God has comforted us and walked with us, and
soul,

Our God is full of compassion. . . .
When I was in great need, he saved me.
e at rest once more, O my soul,
for the LORD has been good to you.
(Psalm 116:5-7)

TS IN CONNECTING WITH GOD
ctices to Consider)

od's compassion within you

ad aloud Psalm 139:1-5 and after each main phrase,
ne: "and God has compassion on me!" Repeat this so
e saying it to God. If you wish, continue with verses
same way.

l Luke 7:11-16 and picture it happening. Write down

anew. As a regular discipline, I need t

Weeping in Prayer. Our "don't
cally avoids the Scripture passages t
help us pray as part of our work in
suffer. I stumbled into doing this af
lion women and children held capt
try each year — how they are lured,
into bondage. I found myself unab
when the order of my daily *lectio*
Psalm 56. Picturing myself as a you
unknown to her and violently be
tion, I prayed in her place for her:

By the
myself call
Help her th
courageous
mies 'retrea
them for the
the waiting
ones who d

Embrac
constantly li
only because
necting with
celebrating h
saying to our

Be gracious to me, O
all day long foes
my enemies trample
for many fight
O Most High, wher
I put my trust i
In God, whose wo
in God I trust
what can flesh
All day long they
all their thou
They stir up strif
they watch n
As they hoped t
so repay them f
in wrath ca
You have kept
put my tea
Are they n
Then my ener

B

EXPERIMEN
(Spiritual Pra

To RECEIVE G

Celebration: Re
add this o
that you'r
13-15 the
Meditation: Rea

the feelings you would have had if you had been the mother or the son. Jot down anything else about Jesus that comes to you.

Study: Read these passages about Jesus being "troubled": John 11:33; 12:27; 13:21. What do they tell you about Jesus?

Worship: Address Jesus, either by writing in a journal or speaking, about the depth of his compassion.

To BECOME one who offers the compassion of Jesus to others

Associating with the lowly: Get into a conversation with someone who needs food (in front of a convenience store, at a soup kitchen). Talk to that person and find out what is charming about her or him. Listen for his or her greatest need. If the person doesn't have food, offer to buy it and share.

Chastity: Consider ways you use people for diversion or even entertainment. What might you pray for them instead?

Fasting: Before fasting, ask God to show you a need you could pray for as you fast. Then fast (even one meal is fine) and use every hunger pang to pray for that need.

Frugality: Go without something you'd like to have but don't need. Devote that money or time to someone in need.

Intercessory prayer: Consider two or three conversations you've had with people and write down their names and their needs.

Listening prayer and intercessory prayer: Ask God to help you learn to hear the cries of people's souls (see Matthew 9:36). Ponder whose souls God is asking you to hear the cries of, perhaps by reading the newspaper or a missions magazine.

Practicing the presence of God: Be mindful of any slight nudge of compassion in the next few days and follow it up by doing something. Don't let it go by in apathy.

Prayer: Pray Psalm 56 for someone who is suffering.

Reflection: Remember the times you have received nudges from God. Did you follow up on them? If so, did you sense the rightness of such follow-up? What are you learning about whether your nudges from God are genuine?

Service and intercessory prayer: Consider the people you serve or serve alongside. Pray for the needs you see in them.

Service and practicing the presence of God: In whatever ways you now serve, pray for the people you serve as you serve them. What does God lead you to pray?

Study: Read the newspaper and look for stories of people who are suffering. What is the cause? What does this lead you to want to pray?

QUESTIONS FOR DISCUSSION AND REFLECTION

1. If you had been one of the disciples walking into Nain with Jesus as he raised the boy to life, how would you have responded?

2. Whom do you know who seems routinely compassionate — compassion is normal or typical for her or him? Describe the ways this person expresses compassion. Reflect on that person.

3. Which of these potential obstacles weaken your compassion for someone?
   - Being interrupted (as Jesus was to heal others)
   - Being confronted with someone who terrifies you or disgusts you
   - Trying to help someone with either extreme disfigurement or insurmountable grief
   - Too many needs with too few resources
   - Other

4. Which do you need more of in your life: prayer or action? What might that look like for you?

5. Which of the experiments listed do you see yourself trying out this week?

7   Tough but Tender

Was Jesus ever angry? Would a Savior so full of compassion also be angry?

Many people claim he was angry, and they seem pleased by this. They think it makes Jesus more human and more approachable. Others, especially those who as children experienced adults' ferocious anger, hope Jesus wasn't.

It's important to set aside what we hope is true and look carefully at the gospel texts, because the truth is both more nuanced and more marvelous than this. For example, most people assume Jesus was angry when he cleansed the temple (see Matthew 21:12-17; Mark 11:15-18; Luke 19:45-46; John 2:13-17). None of the texts, however, say he was angry or mention his feelings or tone of voice. Some say that his using a whip is a clue that he was angry, but would Jesus vent anger on animals by beating them, or did he use the whip as a way to move them along?

A better clue to Jesus' disposition is the worshipful response from the weaker people in the situation: "The blind and the lame came to him at the temple, and he healed them. But when the chief priests and the teachers of the law saw the wonderful things he did and the children shouting in the temple area, 'Hosanna to the Son of David,' they were indignant" (Matthew 21:14-15). The blind (who couldn't see the commotion) and the lame (who couldn't flee) were not frightened by Jesus' throwing over the tables of the moneychangers and driving out the animals. Instead they were drawn to him to be healed. The children, who would have naturally been afraid, were so mesmerized they sang again the song they'd sung as he entered Jerusalem. The only persons described as "indignant" were the chief priests and the teachers of the law.

If, indeed, this scene portrays the anger of Jesus, his anger is very different from ours. Jesus' attitude, demeanor, and behavior resulted in people being healed and praising God. My anger has never resulted in people being healed or praising God.

JESUS-STYLE ANGER

Most instructive is the only instance in the Gospels in which it's explicitly stated that Jesus was angry (Mark 3:1-6). Put yourself in the synagogue crowd in Capernaum and try to picture the scene. A man stands there with a withered arm. He seems to be stationed there by the Pharisees "so that they might accuse him" (3:2, NRSV; see also 2:26). They'd already disapproved of Jesus for healing on the Sabbath because their traditions considered healing to be work, which was prohibited. So they viewed Jesus as a renegade preacher.

Caught in this trap, what does Jesus do? Instead of ignoring the disabled man (something Jesus *wouldn't* do), he calls the man up front. Then he addresses everyone else (most likely the Pharisees) and asks, "Is it lawful to do good or to do harm on the sabbath, to save life or to kill?" (verse 4, NRSV). Ever the teacher, Jesus asks them if the deep goodness of the perfect law of God urges us to heal a disfigured person or ignore him. Is God a life-giver or a life-minimizer? But they are silent.

Then Jesus looks "around at them in anger . . . deeply distressed at their stubborn hearts" (verse 5). The stated reason behind Jesus' anger is his grief at their stubbornness or "hardness of heart" (NRSV). He isn't upset because the religious leaders continually harp at him or because they thwart his ministry (as we would be). He isn't angry because they use this handicapped man. He is angry because of the wretched condition of their hearts. What they are doing to themselves with their long-cultivated hardness of heart grieves him.

In this moment of grieving anger, Jesus tells the man to stretch out his hand, and as he does so, it is healed. Think of all the things this no-longer-disabled man can now do differently with his right hand (see Luke 6:6): earn a living, hug his wife, hold his baby, play an instrument, repair his living space. What is now normal for him was not normal before.

The Pharisees' response to this glorious event is not joy but to "plot with the Herodians how they might kill Jesus" (Mark 3:6). It's at this point that we would expect the text to say, "and then Jesus got really mad." If your life has ever been threatened, you know the fear, defensiveness, and anger that comes. But anger is not mentioned now. Apparently Jesus didn't take death threats personally. How can that be? We take nearly everything personally.

The Focused Heart

The unusual anger of Jesus rested in his grief over the state of others' souls, in this case, the hardness of the Pharisees' hearts. This makes sense because Jesus loved his enemies; he wanted what was best for them, even the Pharisees (see Luke 6:27,35). They were destroying their connection with God and others' connection with God through their influence. These Pharisees had "rejected God's purpose for themselves" (Luke 7:30).

Jesus' way of being angry involves loving people by focusing on what is best for them. He labored for the restoration of people's souls and wanted that for the Pharisees. That is so different from most human anger. Our way of being angry with people does not involve having a heart focused on loving them. We don't think about what

God intended for them and how tragic it is that they're missing the mark. We think, *You're wrong; you're hurting me (or others). Stop it!*

The Clean Heart

Another unusual feature of Jesus' anger is his cleanness of heart. While we become bitter or defensive or "talk trash" about people, Jesus did not. He took nothing personally, even their death threats. He is like the Father: "For I am God, and not man — the Holy One among you. I will not come in wrath" (Hosea 11:9). Our Trinitarian God doesn't have temper tantrums but delights in showing mercy (see Micah 7:18).

This is so different from human anger that we cannot fathom it. When we get angry, we think unkind thoughts and may even yell and want to punch people or take the quieter route of smoldering and sulking and avoiding. Do we *assume* Jesus was harsh and mean when angry because we are?

The Compassionate Heart

But, you might protest, wasn't Jesus angry when he scolded the Pharisees (see Matthew 23:1-37)? There he reproached them for their pride in wanting to be applauded, their willingness to show off with religious duties, and their hypocrisy in emphasizing miniscule details but missing the big picture of who God is: justice, mercy, and faithfulness. His words do not seem gentle — at least *not yet* — but perhaps his words were grieving and mournful, for he says, "Woe to you" seven times, which can also be translated, "Alas for you," an expression of grief. Did he tenderly hold one of their faces in his hands as he said, "Alas for you"?

But explicitly gentle words do come at the end of the scolding: "O Jerusalem, Jerusalem, you who kill the prophets and stone those sent to you, how often I have longed to gather your children together, as a hen gathers her chicks under her wings, but you were not willing" (Matthew 23:37). He longs not to smack them around but to cradle and protect them. Why? N. T. Wright explained this image to us urban dwellers. When a fire enters a barnyard, a mother hen gathers the chicks under her spread-out wings and bows her head low over them to protect them. After the fire is extinguished, the farmer finds the mother hen still bent over but dead and the chicks alive under her wings.[1] This sacrificial mother image is the picture of what Jesus would be doing within a few weeks on the cross. He wanted to give Israel shelter, rest, protection, and blessing; but would they accept it? Perhaps he wept as he said these things, as he had done when saying similar things a few days earlier as he approached the city of Jerusalem, stopping to look over it (see Luke 19:41; see also Luke 13:34-35).

Still, you may wonder, what about how Jesus calls the Pharisees a "brood of vipers"? Isn't that sarcastic name-calling? Consider that the context suggests deep sympathy instead of cynicism. This passage introduces the Matthew 23–25 sermon, which predicts the destruction of Jerusalem. Keep in mind that Jesus used the familiar image of spreading fire in 23:37. When you combine the images of snakes and wildfire, you get an image familiar to readers because in the desert, groups of snakes flee together in front of a fire that flows like a river behind them as if it is chasing them. (In fire country where I live, it isn't unusual to see deer, coyotes, squirrels, and especially snakes fleeing down a hillside in front of a fire, trying to escape it.) Again, the fire in this case was the future of the Jewish people: being trapped in the city of Jerusalem as the Roman armies destroyed it. Many of these listeners would not escape unless they followed Jesus' advice to flee to the hills (see Matthew 24:16). Here Jesus warns them of this upcoming destruction as he does so many other times: "All this will come upon this generation" (Matthew 23:36).

Consider that Jesus' style of anger was not mean, but drenched with compassion. To have a compassionate heart when angry means we mourn the harm that others' anger does to their own souls.

If it's difficult for you to imagine Jesus having a loving heart when angry, you're not alone. Most of us have not experienced such behavior, and so we can't imagine Jesus doing this. The way of Jesus — the deepest sort of love, joy, and peace as he combined the toughness of justice and truth with the tenderness of love and mercy — is foreign to us. For Jesus, tenderness did not mean weakness as it often does for us. Even in the midst of proclaiming and implementing justice, he would not break a bruised reed or snuff out a smoldering wick. For Jesus, toughness did not require quarreling, screaming, and violence (see Matthew 12:18-21). Living out of the kingdom of God, Jesus had a tender heart even toward those whose hearts were hard.

PAYING ATTENTION WITH GOD TO OUR ANGER

Does having the focused, clean, and compassionate heart of Christ seem impossible to you? If so, recall that we *share in* the life of Christ, so we can ask him to help us be attentive to our anger in his safe presence. In that context of mutual abiding in Christ, we can process our anger in God's presence and look at what's behind it to tap more deeply into that life of Christ. This is how an interactive life with God works.

Paying such attention, however, is the opposite of our natural inclinations. Many people bury anger and pretend it's not there, but feelings thrive when buried alive. Other people vent their anger on others, ignoring what Jesus said about anger being the root of so much destruction in our lives that he tells us to urgently interrupt whatever we're doing to address it (see Matthew 5:23-26).

What does it look like to be attentive to our anger within the safe, loving circle of the Trinitarian presence? Many avenues are possible, but the first step is to *walk away* from the person or situation that angers us. It's urgent that we do not speak, because what we say will do harm to the person. Even if we say the truth, our anger taints the truth so it's not heard. Yet we're not withdrawing forever. We can say to a rebellious teenager, "We'll discuss it when I'm not angry" or to a coworker, "I'll be ready to talk about this in an hour." If nothing else, we can excuse ourselves to use the restroom! It's better to do this than to injure another person's fragile soul.

In this time apart, we can ask God to show us what we need to do to process the anger. Here are a few options.

Confess it to God. Tell God about your anger, perhaps even writing about it in a journal. (You can destroy it later if necessary.) Don't beat yourself up, but state what is wrong and what you think your part in it is. If you're unable to do this, try this next course of action.

Pray the gut-level psalms. Say to God exactly what is going on inside you. God can bear to hear it. Prayer is not along the lines of what Thumper's mother said to Thumper in the book and movie *Bambi*: "If you can't say [pray] something nice, don't say [pray] anything at all." God has heard it all before in Psalms 58, 69, 109, 129, 137, and 140. In fact, you may want to use these psalms to form your words.

As you vent, ponder the shifts that occur in these psalms. Some end with abrupt praise. Others shift from ranting to listing all the psalmist is grateful for. In Psalm 139, the psalmist moved from blood-curdling phrases and homicidal tirade ("If only you would slay the wicked, O God! . . . Do I not hate those who hate you, O LORD, and abhor those who rise up against you?" verses 19,21) to "Search me, O God, and know my heart; test me and know my anxious thoughts. See if there is any offensive way in me, and lead me in the way everlasting" (verses 23-24). The psalmist moved from others to self. Twelve-step groups phrase it this way: "I stay on my side of the street; I let you stay on your side." Instead of ranting about how messy the other side of the street is, the psalmist returns to his own side, also messy. Such honest praying often ends wisely with self-examination: Search me! Perhaps King David was enabled to behave honorably toward Saul (who had tried to kill him many times) because he prayed these imprecatory prayers for which he is credited. Did Jesus perhaps pray them as well?

Attempt to pray with a right heart. As soon as you are able, ask God to give you a *focused heart,* a *clean heart,* and a *compassionate heart.* See what happens. Awhile ago I found myself deeply annoyed with a Christian who was unkind and spiteful toward a non-Christian whom I often talked with about spiritual things. How could this much-looked-up-to Christian act with such venom while wearing the name of Jesus? Yet I felt guilty about my inability to love her. While hiking one day, I plopped down on the side of the trail under a willow tree in frustration but then remembered Benedictine John Chapman's words: "Pray as you can, not as you can't."[2] This means we focus on what we can do instead of what we can't do.

What could I do? Matthew 5:44 came to mind about loving and praying for enemies. This Christian wasn't my enemy, but I could apply it just as well to a friend. But, love her? I didn't want to. As I sat there, it came to me that loving and praying is plan A (what I couldn't do), but to simply pray for her would be plan B (what I could do). In the shelter of those tree limbs, I tried plan B. But what to pray for her? A *focused heart* would pray what was best for her, so I used Philippians 1:9-10: that her love would abound more and more; that her knowledge and discernment would increase. After a few months of praying that (and learning to mean it), I began to be able to speak kindly to her again and found I genuinely cared about what happened in her life. The *clean* and *compassionate heart* eventually followed.

Ask, what is this anger really about? In an attempt to pray with a clean heart, I had to ask God, *What is within my heart toward this woman?* Sometimes I was afraid of her. Often anger is rooted in fear; anger becomes our armor of protection when we are afraid. If I'm afraid of being walked on, I might protect myself by speaking with anger. So when angry, it's wise to ask, *What am I afraid of? What are my long-forgotten fears? How am I afraid I won't be loved or valued in*

Selfish anger is not God's anger.

this situation? How do I feel I must protect myself to get what I need?

Other times, anger is about pride. We really want to have our own way, so we try to control the person or situation. We want this person to give us the love and value we feel we deserve, even the credit he or she won't give us. Arguing and pushing has seemed the only way to get my way.

Ask God to show you your next step. In this time-out we see the situation more clearly and make wiser decisions. Perhaps you need to state simply to the other person what you need. Perhaps the individual crossed your boundaries because you never stated them.

As we process our anger in God's company, the central issue is usually needing to trust God more. Anger seems necessary only when we're not sure God will help us. Then I try to be my own shepherd and meet my own needs. An all-important task is to keep steeping ourselves in the reality of an eternal life with God. In that reality, I can lie down in green pastures because I'm protected by God. I don't have to be up on all four feet claiming my territory and shooing away intruders. I can trust that God will find green pastures tomorrow and still waters next week (see Psalm 23:1-2). I can feel safe with God.

So is it okay to be angry?

Yes, it's okay to be angry, but process your anger in God's company and see what God says to you. Ask God to give you a *focused heart* — wanting what's best for the person you're angry with. Ask God for a *clean heart* — one that refuses to be bitter or mean or defensive. Ask God for a *compassionate heart* — mourning the harm this person is doing to self.

You may wonder if anger can't sometimes be good, especially righteous indignation. We think it's all right because we're angry for a good cause. But does it help? Consider Moses killing an Egyptian to deliver a Hebrew slave. This didn't fulfill God's purpose of delivering Israel. Instead Israel resented Moses, and he got kicked out of town, which may have delayed his mission.

Righteous indignation usually has no long-lasting effect. In the moment, people are impressed (or so annoyed they dismiss you). But their hearts and minds are not changed because you bullied them. The tender kingdom heart is the persuasive one. Still, if you're sure you're called to show your righteous indignation, consider processing it all with God first. If you have worked at having a focused heart, a clean heart, and a compassionate heart, you probably won't speak with indignation at all but with a generous heart full of tenderness that will amaze your listener (and you!).

An instance in which anger can help you is when you're sick and tired of being sick and tired of something you keep doing. Even then, process the situation before God and let God lead you to take the next step that you've needed to take for a long time. In that case, anger can create godly sorrow in you, which leaves no regret. It can then produce in you earnestness, longing, and a readiness to see you do justice (see 2 Corinthians 7:10).

But it's tricky. Anger is helpful *only if* we process it with God. Then the results will be love, compassion, and respect. Several years ago I rejected the following idea but have since decided it is right: "there is nothing that can be done with anger that can't be done better without it."[3] It's better to leave anger to God. Jesus was able to go into the temple with a whip. Don't trust me with one.

WHERE TO START

Timely

As you look at the spiritual disciplines that follow, consider especially the role of solitude and silence. The apostle Paul had been an angry person — breathing threats of violence, destroying the church, and dragging men and women off to prison (see Acts 9:1; 8:3). He needed three years of solitude in Arabia.

Consider also situational silences, such as choosing not to have "the last word" in a conversation. We want to explain further — if they just understood! We especially want to have the final word when we've been put down. Not having the last word creates inner peace when someone tries to get a reaction from us or offers a final zinger. Can I let the comment stand? Can I not defend myself against a put-down? Can I trust that the Lord is my shepherd in this situation? To be silent means we don't have to compete—to top the other person or prove our point.

When I first tried it, it seemed impossible. But then I saw my sweet sister do it when a family member smarted off to her. I felt myself become irritated at the family member, but my sister said nothing. Instead, she grinned at the family member.

What happened next was dynamic. The look on the family member's face melted. She realized she'd been unkind to my sister, who was always kind to her and even in that moment stood there smiling at her. Next, I, who stood off to the side, felt my irritation vanish as God's grace (in my sister's grin) poured over me also. This grace-drenched silence began with my sister's "grace grin." In that silence, I was able to love instead of be angry. Since then, I've used her grace grin to help me not have the last word. (It helps to do *something* with your mouth.) I've been amazed how it hasn't been phony. Somehow as my mouth grins, I can feel myself moving toward having that focused heart, clean heart, and compassionate heart.

EXPERIMENTS IN CONNECTING WITH GOD
(Spiritual Practices to Consider)

To RECEIVE this tender kingdom heart from God

Meditation: Read Mark 3:1-6 and picture it happening. Write down the feelings you would have had if you had been the man with the withered arm. How do you feel about Jesus? What do you wish to tell him?

Meditation: Picture yourself in Psalm 23:5. God is standing behind you, anointing you with oil to show how special you are.

Across from you is an "enemy" (anyone you find difficult today). Notice how God keeps filling your cup because this everyday enemy upsets you. God is not going to leave you but keeps anointing you and making sure your needs are met to overflowing.

To BECOME one who offers this tender kingdom heart to difficult people

Confession: Tell God about the last time you were angry. What was behind it? What is the core issue plaguing you? What is your next step?

Fasting: Abstain from all food for a meal or two or from eating something you really like. Journal about how it feels not to have what you want. Write about what it would mean to be quite content not having those things — to be strong and cheerful when not getting your way.

Fasting: Abstain as just described but focus especially on relying on God for everything — to be energetic, kind, and content while hungry.

Meditation: Meditate on (and even memorize) Psalm 23. Say it back to God with a sense that any day now you will actually believe it.

Prayer: Ask God to show you your next step in having a clean heart, focused heart, and compassionate heart toward someone you find difficult. Journal about how the soul of someone you find difficult needs to be restored.

Prayer: Practice gut-level prayer (you may use one of the imprecatory psalms listed earlier), beating on the floor if you have to, telling God how angry or fearful you are. Commit yourself to let God search your heart.

Recollection: Look over today and yesterday. To whom did you speak with a tender kingdom heart? How does it feel to treat people that way?

Silence: Journal about people with whom you might try not having the last word. What will you do instead? Try it.

Solitude: Spend some time away from others, doing nothing. Hang out with God. Rest your soul. If nothing else, walk in the park.

QUESTIONS FOR DISCUSSION AND REFLECTION

1. Describe the expression you imagine to have been on Jesus' face as he looked at the Pharisees in anger and grieved over their hardness of heart.
2. Pick a situation in which you feel thwarted (and then angry). Which sort of heart would be the most accessible for you:
   - A focused heart (wanting what's best for the person)?
   - A clean heart (not being bitter or taking things personally)?
   - A compassionate heart (having compassion for this person)?
3. What might keep you from walking away when you're angry?
4. Can you see yourself using a ranting prayer? If so, when and where?
5. Which of the experiments listed are you most likely to try out (perhaps innovate)?

8   Speaking the Truth in Love

Anger, especially when buried, is elusive. It can bubble to the surface out of nowhere. One minute you're the normal person you know yourself to be and the next minute you're surprised by what comes out of your mouth. Road rage and snapping at children happen before you have time to think. So we ask, How can we control our mouth better?

Yet it isn't really a question of the mouth or circumstances. The mouth can respond only according to what has been cultivated in the heart: "The good man brings good things out of the good stored up in his heart, and the evil man brings evil things out of the evil stored up in his heart. For out of the overflow of his heart his mouth speaks" (Luke 6:45). The thoughts, feelings, and intentions we have stored up within us leak. If we bury negative currents, they betray themselves in the knit of the eyebrows or the angle of the shoulders.

Spur-of-the-moment anger that seizes us — usually because we're surprised — is typically fed from a pool of underlying contempt. Most people are unaware that they have fed this pool for years and that it affects so much of their life. Because we live off this reservoir of contempt, it doesn't work to tell ourselves, *I won't get mad this time* or to implement six handy anger management tips.

*   As we process with God the contempt within us, we become the
kind of people inside who don't get angry. We focus our life on the
kingdom of God here and now, cultivating a compassionate heart
and rooting out the contempt that creeps outward from our inner
self to the people and circumstances around us.

WHAT IS CONTEMPT?

Contempt is studied anger. It percolates from the brooding that
occurs when doing otherwise normal things such as mowing the
lawn or vacuuming. In these moments, the mind drifts to how we've
been mistreated. When contempt is a routine thought pattern, it
seeps into all of life as chronic grumbling and even bitterness. At the
drop of a hat, hostility emerges ("That stupid bus driver!").

Observable contempt shows itself in sarcasm (that word is derived
from "tearing the flesh"), name-calling ("Elitist snob! Flaming fun-
damentalist!"), and forceful speech that gets louder and more harsh.
It leaks into cynicism ("That will never work for me.") and rejection
of authority.

Contempt in its subtle forms shows up in perfectionism ("I'll
show my dad!"), playing the victim ("Poor me."), and procrastina-
tion. If contempt is hidden under those layers of your otherwise
pleasant self, it may slip out most easily with people whose eyes
you can't see. For years, I struggled to be kind to telemarketers.
They seemed to call when I was in deep concentration on my work
or waiting for an important telephone call. When I answered the
phone and the caller wanted to sell me carpeting, I responded with
irritation, not considering that this innocent person was just trying
to make a living.

If you're unaware of contempt within you, recall a photo of yourself caught "off guard" (against what?). What were you thinking? Our
faces reveal that reservoir of contempt with narrowed eyes or rolling
eyes, with sneering or a curled lip. Most of what we communicate is

not through words but through facial expressions, gestures, and tone of voice. That's why our children pick up our worst attitudes that we carefully try to shield them from. They see and hear it, but not always in words.

Contempt Is Now Acceptable

Consider how society accepts contempt in most talk radio shows. Even on the milder ones, people agree with each other saying, "I can't believe anyone would really . . ." (a politer way of saying others just don't know as much as we do). It's acceptable to put down anyone who doesn't agree with us on politics, the environment, or eating meat. On Christian talk shows, compartmentalizing and disparaging people seem okay because we're right and they're wrong. But can political or theological bashing ever be right? Consider this wise warning—to "beware of believing that it is okay for us to condemn as long as we are condemning the right things"[1] for the right reasons.

Contempt works in such a way that if we think we're right, we slip into moral superiority that says, *I'm not only right; I'm better than you.* Religious contempt expresses itself with thoughts such as, *At least I'm not like . . .* , as expressed by the Pharisee in Jesus' parable who "trusted in themselves that they were righteous and regarded others with contempt," including the humble tax collector next to him (Luke 18:9, NRSV).

Contempt is deemed acceptable if you're stressed, even in the workaholic Christian worker: "Don't be offended. She's under a lot of stress right now."

Perhaps the most culturally acceptable form of contempt is the pet peeve. Think about it: We *choose* to dislike and discredit certain people we don't know and have never met because of one small thing they do that we find annoying. These people are then exempt from the "love clause" in Scripture—the Great Commandment; they're people we don't *have to* love.

For children of the light—called to light the world—a

life-rhythm of everyday hostility is a serious problem. In the Sermon on the Mount Jesus taught about anger and contempt first and then about marriage (see Matthew 5:21-30) because anger and contempt are what often ruin a marriage (and all relationships). Even if divorce is deemed necessary, the scars will be less if it is carried out without contempt (see verses 31-32). To live free of contempt makes it easier to bless enemies, to never retaliate, and to never condemn others (see verses 39-48; 7:1-6).

THE TENDER KINGDOM HEART

What would such a life look like? Mean-spiritedness did not erupt from Jesus because contempt was not in him, as clearly evidenced on the night of his arrest. When threatened with arrest, some people become so angry they lead car chases and shoot at the police. Indeed, the Roman soldiers who joined the temple police the night of Jesus' arrest did not expect an easy task. They came equipped with lanterns and torches, apparently imagining they'd have to search in caves and crevices of the walls of the garden. They brought weapons to trap this itinerant preacher who had never, as far as we know, wielded a sword (John 18:3).

Picture Jesus' serenity as the chief priests who had taunted him and plotted to kill him now stand before him (see Luke 22:52). Free of contempt or scorn, he doesn't call them names or breathe out threats. He isn't sarcastic or cynical, saying, "I knew you'd show up eventually." He shows no sign of agitation or turmoil. "A peace and calm which is beyond the world possess Him. . . . His extreme gentleness of manner is marvelous . . . full of *dignity* and *measured reason* which is *more effective than hot wrath*. The majesty of heaven shines out in every word and deed in this hour of humiliation."[2]

Such calm would not have been possible if Jesus had brooded over the chief priests' self-important attitudes or dwelt on the words of their death threats as he went to sleep every night. Out of his focused, clean, and compassionate love for the chief priests, the scribes, the Pharisees, the Roman soldiers, and the crowd — all responsible for his death — he said, "Father, forgive them; they don't know what they're doing" (Luke 23:34, MSG).

Truth Drenched in Love

Jesus responded with love and serenity at this stressful moment because he trusted God and lived within that life of God (see John 13:31; 15:9; 17:22-23). For you and me, it involves a retraining of the entire self so drenched in a culture of contempt. When that self is retrained, it can easily speak the truth in love (see Ephesians 4:15).

Consider how Jesus speaks the truth in love to Judas, who kisses him and says, "Greetings, Rabbi!" In love Jesus addresses Judas as "friend" but also states the hard truth to "do what you came for" (Matthew 26:50). When Peter slices off the ear of the high priest's slave, Jesus in love heals the poor slave but turns to Peter to present hard-to-swallow truth: "Do you think I cannot call on my Father, and he will at once put at my disposal more than twelve legions of angels? But how then would the Scriptures be fulfilled that say it must happen in this way?" (Matthew 26:53-54).

Jesus' question to the crowd presents truth in an almost teasing, playful way: "Am I leading a rebellion, that you have come out with swords and clubs to capture me? Every day I sat in the temple courts teaching, and you did not arrest me. But this has all taken place that the writings of the prophets might be fulfilled" (Matthew 26:55-56). He is asking them, "Do you see that I'm *letting* you take me? (as he had *not* let them do before; see Luke 4:30; John 7:32-36,45-46; 8:59; 11:57).

Speaking the truth in love is one of the most difficult things to do. Most of us are either eager prophetic truth tellers or nicer sentimentalists who skip the truth. The former usually speak truth in pride or anger: "I'm sorry; that's what the Bible says" or "Somebody had to tell him!" The latter lie in love: "I don't mind driving five hundred miles out of my way to bring you your lunch." Both may have good intentions, but truth tellers end up speaking the truth with contempt, and contempt withers the soul.[3] The latter can't be trusted because in their niceness they don't mean what they say and they can't be depended upon to follow through.

Truth Without Love

Speaking truth *without* love does more harm than good because people tune you out. Any truth you tried to speak is cloaked in pride or harshness, which is all listeners hear. Many people see God as mean and harsh because they've heard truths about God spoken this way. To use contemptuous, pushy, or harsh language is to try to force their will (or heart or spirit), that deep part of them that makes them who they are. Words become swords and spears to prod, convince, and manipulate.

To speak the truth without contempt means that I show respect for people — if not for themselves, then for them as people God *so loves.* Contempt-free truth is spoken without moral superiority or exaggerated opinions about oneself, without boasting or presuming to know the entire situation.

Kent Groff made this last point by telling about when he was leading a series of Sunday morning workshops for a congregation. While attending the worship service, he noticed a row of teens sitting together. One young man wore a baseball cap in church. Kent, usually very accepting, wondered how this kid could be so disrespectful.

Afterward at fellowship time, Kent observed the boy repositioning the cap on his much-scarred bare scalp and figured out the truth: "This was Chris — and I had actually been praying for him. He had sustained a head injury from a car crash and was undergoing multiple surgeries. In a moment my judgmental mind-set was turned upside down."[4] Kent easily presumed he knew the truth about Chris and then condemned (judged) him, if only in his mind. Presumption is always dangerous because only God knows all.

Judgment: Discernment Versus Condemnation

The English word *judge* is used to mean two different things in the New Testament. One meaning is to "discern,"[5] which is to examine things and get details, to weigh issues and to determine the excellence of something. Love helps us discern (see Philippians 1:10). But *judge* can also mean "condemn"[6] (see Matthew 7:1; James 4:11; Romans 14:4,13). Condemnation involves moral superiority as we look down on others. For the person living out of the kingdom of God, truth can be spoken with discernment but never in condemnation. Even Jesus did not come into the world to condemn the world but to save it (see John 3:17), but we somehow think it's okay if we do it. "But it's the truth!" we protest. In reality, condemnation is never my job but God's.

To speak truth with discernment instead of condemnation takes thought, prayer, and practice. Several years ago, I found myself annoyed with my twentysomething son after telling him about how one of my favorite clients at the Samaritan Center had been injured. While my client-friend was drunk one night and wandering in the street, he had been hit by a car, thrown up in the air, and then hit again as he descended. He was in the hospital unconscious with broken bones and internal injuries. My otherwise delightful son responded immediately by saying that's what happened to the main character in the movie *Meet Joe Black*. How could he compare my client-friend to a stunt man and mannequin who had escaped unhurt? How insensitive! I was irritated and walked away. But as I stepped away, I asked God to help me have a focused heart (wanting my son to be a more sensitive person), a clean heart (not thinking about other times he may have done this), and a compassionate heart (knowing his future wife would wish this). I felt I should say something to my son about this, but I didn't yet have the right heart. It would have come out condemning.

As I hiked the next day, I meditated on 1 Corinthians 13. (When I do this, I change the words a little so that verses 4-8 say, *God* is patient, *God* is kind, and so on, instead of *love* is patient and *love* is kind. I usually come away in majestic worship of how great God is, also knowing that God's sort of love will somehow leak into me and change me as whatever we meditate on usually does.) On that day, part of me was also rehearsing how I might speak the truth in love to my son about this insensitivity: Could I speak the truth with patience? With kindness? Without envying? Boasting? Being proud? Being rude (pushy) or self-seeking (trying to prove my point!)? Without being easily irritated? Could I speak truth but always protect him (see verses 4-7)?

As I headed home, I confessed to God I could not speak the truth in love to my son. If I tried, I'd speak it with a little contempt, and that would not be protecting him. He's dear to me, my near-clone on earth. How could I do that to him? So I asked God to help *someone else* speak the truth to him. (I don't take this prayer lightly. I've been praying for ten years for God to do this with someone to whom I could not speak the truth in love.)

Later that day, my son came into my office, and we began laughing about something he told me. As we chatted, I found myself saying gently, "That's how I felt yesterday when you made that comment about our client who was hurt being like the movie *Meet Joe Black*." My son looked at me in puzzlement and slight horror and apologized. I had not spoken with contempt, and he had heard me without injury. In meditation and prayer, I had done my connecting with God, and God mysteriously did the perfecting in me before I realized it.

The *act* of speaking the truth doesn't condemn someone; it's *how* we speak truth that condemns and communicates contempt. It's possible to disagree quite agreeably if we are not people who must have our own way.

Starter Disciplines

In chapter 3 we talked about not giving one's opinion unless asked. After trying this, I noticed that if I didn't even bother to form an opinion, this would train me to discern instead of to judge. For example, I refuse to evaluate a sermon. Instead as I listen I ponder these questions, which are written in the front of my Bible: What do I need to learn that I have missed? What is God saying to me today? This helps me stay on my side of the street — the preacher didn't ask my opinion, after all.

Another exercise that helps in speaking the truth in love is *retraining the body*. During an exercise of dedicating the body,[7] I realized that my body muscles and gestures communicated contempt. So I tried standing before a mirror and reflecting judgment and love with each body part. I was shocked to see that I could communicate love instead of contempt with the arch of my eyebrows, the way I held my arms, and the set of my mouth. (See exercise, "self-examination.")

Besides retraining oneself out of behaviors that impart contempt, it's wise to look at who I condemn in my heart and do this on a regular basis. To help myself *become aware of contempt and condemnation*, I use the following exercise (based on James 4:11-12 and Matthew 5:38-42).

Shut your eyes and imagine yourself in a courtroom. The defendant is someone who should be on trial because he or she has done a few things wrong to you or someone you love. Try to let God choose this person for you. This might be anyone you're angry with, mildly frustrated with, or feel contempt for. (Take a minute to do this.)

Get the setting in your mind. Then look around the courtroom. Where are you? (Pause to find yourself.)

If you're in the seat of the judge or the prosecutor or the jury or the witness stand, try to get up and sit in a neutral seat with the spectators.

If you're hiding in the back of the courtroom or even out in the lobby, come and sit in a neutral seat with the spectators. (Pause again to get settled.)

Now take a deep breath. Try to imagine yourself getting up out of your seat and going to sit in the row of chairs behind the accused.

These are reserved for the dear friends of the accused. Even if you can't sit there very long, try it for a few seconds. If you're simply not able, ask Jesus to sit there for you.[8]

What does this make you want to pray?

Cultivating a heart that trusts God with people we might otherwise have contempt for transforms the soul. As we align ourselves minute by minute with the One who is consistently kind even to the ungrateful, our character starts to take on the character *of* his Son. Such a life is lived from an unseen kingdom.

EXPERIMENTS IN CONNECTING WITH GOD
(Spiritual Practices to Consider)

To RECEIVE this truthful way of loving from God

Meditation: Read John 18:1-11. Now shut your eyes and picture the scene. Read it again and see what words engage you and where you find yourself in the crowd: a disciple? a soldier? a temple police official who has tried to arrest Jesus several times before? What are your thoughts and feelings, especially about Jesus? What do you need to say to Jesus? Write that down and address Jesus. If you have words of worship, be sure to offer those as well.

Meditation: Picture Zephaniah 3:17: God's quieting you with his love and singing over you. Rest in this. Then picture God quieting someone you love dearly. Rest in this. Then picture God quieting someone you barely know (a clerk at the store, a neighbor you've only passed). Rest in this. Then picture God quieting someone for whom you have held contempt. Rest in this.

To BECOME one who loves in a truthful way

Confession: Confess your routine ways of showing contempt, using these questions if needed:

Where do I have a sense of superiority?

Whom do I wish to control?

Whom do I criticize most?

Fasting: Give up sweets for two days and see if you can still be nice to people.

Fellowship: Discuss with a friend your pet peeves and how you have let them block relationships. (Or journal about this.)

Meditation: Meditate on (and even memorize) 1 Corinthians 13, especially verses 4-8 and combine it with Ephesians 4:15 as done above.

Self-examination: Retrain the body. Start with the eyes. Reflect judgment and contempt, then love. Do the same with your shoulders. Then eyebrows (be sure to catch this one in the mirror; it will horrify you), mouth and lips (notice the inside of your mouth — are you sucking your cheeks in?), and stomach. Finally, try saying aloud the word *ketchup* with judgment and contempt. Do it a few times until you get it right. Then try to say it with love.

Silence: Consider the practice of not forming opinions about others. How might this help you? With whom do you especially need to implement it? What freedom might it bring you — especially the freedom to love?

Practicing the presence of God: With whom in your life (a difficult person) might you want to offer this breath prayer as you interact with that person: "Bless ___ through me."

QUESTIONS FOR DISCUSSION AND REFLECTION

1. In what way does contempt leak from you?

sarcasm	name-calling	forceful speech (louder and meaner)
filthy language	grumbling	cynicism
depression	procrastination	rejection of authority
playing the victim	perfectionism	moral superiority
passive-aggressive behavior	withdrawing	pet peeves

2. How would your life be better without contempt?
3. In what situation would it help if you discerned instead of
     judged?
4. Without saying who the defendant was in the courtroom scene,
     tell how willing you were to sit in the chair of the dear friend
     of the accused. If you weren't able to do it, how did you feel
     about Jesus sitting there?
5. Which of the experiments listed are you most likely to try out?

9 Cheerfully Going the Extra Mile

A confession: At times when I've "gone the extra mile" for someone, that mile has seemed exceptionally long. Now and then when I've helped an elderly person clean up her yard or picked up someone late at night or helped people I barely know move, I've labored over this thought: Why am I doing this? There are several reasons for this. Mostly it's because I'm self-absorbed but I tried for once to be noble. Because it was ego-led, it wasn't God-led. The sweetness dried up.

On the other hand, I have done those same tasks and been swept along in the kingdom of God with a heart carefully focused on Jesus, and then the extra mile flew by. I was even having fun. Without self-congratulation, I moved through it as a fly sitting on the tail of the donkey Jesus is riding on. Wherever Jesus went, I was happy to tag along.

Jesus' way of going above and beyond what anyone expects is the kind of thing that attracts people to him. This is how others "know we are Christians by our love," as that song says. It's fighting fire not with fire but with a shocking amount of water. It's overcoming evil with good.

Jesus' greatness of spirit especially radiates in how he went out of his way for people when he was under extreme duress. Ask any woman delivering a baby and she'll tell you that in these times, we can barely be polite much less kind and good and giving. But even on Jesus' way to the cross, he gave to others. When the sympathetic women of Jerusalem came to comfort him, he became the giver and cared for them by warning them to take cover in the hills during the upcoming destruction of Jerusalem (see Luke 23:27-31, referring to 21:20-24). Even more extreme, in his suffering on the cross the first three of his recorded sayings were directed toward the good of others, especially the assigning of his widowed mother, Mary, and the apostle John to one another (see John 19:26-27). Who would benefit more: the poor widow by the wealthier adopted son or the Son of Thunder who would need a contemplative mother (see Luke 2:19,51)?

GOING AN EXTRA MILE WITH *WHOM*?

This idea of going the extra mile is already radical — so selfless, so compassionate — without the extreme detail of whom Jesus had in mind as the recipient of this favor: "If someone forces you to go one mile, go with him two miles" (Matthew 5:41). The only person who could have *forced* one of Jesus' listeners to go an extra mile would have been a Roman soldier. The Romans were the occupying enemy, the pagans that needed to be overthrown, the ones against whom insurrection leaders rose up repeatedly.

I understand I'm to love my enemies, but that means to treat them decently. Does it also mean to bear their burdens for them? After all, it takes so much effort to cultivate a focused heart, clean heart, and compassionate heart. Am I also asked to serve them? To *do good* to those who hate me (see Luke 6:27)?

Perhaps this doesn't bother you because you think you have no real enemies — no one has plotted to kill you lately as they did Jesus.

But this also refers to everyday enemies. Jesus' listeners didn't hate that particular soldier who forced them to go an extra mile. The soldier would have been an annoying nuisance — a nameless person for whom they felt contempt just because he was a Roman. So consider that an enemy can be anyone you're angry with, mildly frustrated with, or struggling with. An enemy might even be like the Roman soldier: someone you don't know but with whom you differ politically; who has power over you that you resent; who comes from a foreign land; who commits your pet peeve. (All that "Hail Caesar" hollering would have offended a Jew.) An enemy can be *anyone you find difficult today, anyone you could like a little more.*

To pray for and work through feelings about everyday enemies is important because it teaches us to cultivate a right heart that is at home in our interactive life with God — a heart that is focused on what's best for people, that is cleansed from bitterness, that naturally flows with compassion. Daily, even minute-by-minute cleanup is wise because someone doesn't become an enemy overnight. It usually happens little by little. (That's why I'm often surprised by whom God brings to my attention when I lead a group in the courtroom scene in the previous chapter.) Diligently keeping one's heart right as each difficult situation comes up enables us to live an eternal life with God now, every minute.

Jesus' best-known parable highlights a predicament of a wise person finding that two people he loves and is close to are, in reality, his enemies at that moment (see Luke 15:11-32). They both oppose him but in different ways. How will he treat them?

This prodigal son story is cherished because it illustrates Jesus' radical extra-mile approach, and we know how much we need for him to go the extra mile for us. Still, it's a shocking story. Forgiving people their wrongs is one thing, but giving them a party is quite another. Yet in Jesus' parable of the son-turned-adversary, the radical father did this. The prodigal son had, after all, proclaimed something close to, "Let's pretend you're dead, Dad. I'll take my half now."

Yet this father quickly pulled together a party after the wayward son returned. Had he been fattening this calf in hope of needing it?

This father (actually, our Father) was an extra-mile walker in so many ways: He watched for years; he ran down the trail to embrace the rebel. He didn't begrudgingly let the boy have a party, but he initiated the celebration and insisted on it. The door of forgiveness was always open, and he eagerly honored a boy who didn't deserve it. This was over-the-top, going a lot of extra miles. (That the boy wanted to come home to be a common worker tells you that the great-hearted father was the star employer of the entire area — his workers always had food to spare. I imagine he also provided good health care, clean places to live, and swing sets for the kids. People must have stood in line to work on his ranch.)

Even more shocking is the father's behavior toward the boy who never left, but who also wronged him with his bitterness. He didn't scold the reluctant son or lock him out. He went to the boy (it should have been the other way around) and stated a truth the older son apparently did not value: "You are always with me, and everything I have is yours" (verse 31). This responsible son had been with the father all that time but had never partied with him before, wrongly viewing the father as a slave master. The parable ends with the father's arms open wide to the older son: What will he do?

Once as I meditated on this passage I saw myself as one of the listening Pharisees (who must have identified themselves in the self-righteous older son). I imagined Jesus taking the role of the magnanimous father, turning and looking at them and opening his arms to them as he said invitationally, "You are always with me. Everything I have is yours." Another time, I was someone who watched the older son and saw in his face the face of one of my relatives who needed endless reassurance. I had resented this about her, but in this story I realized that my reassurance was such a small thing to give her — why was I so stingy? Couldn't I be more generous?

The kingdom of our extra-mile God is pictured by Jesus as a

party — a feast, a marriage feast where there's a lot of laughter and dancing. Yes, we're forgiven, but so much more too. He keeps inviting: "Then he sent some more servants and said, 'Tell those who have been invited that I have prepared my dinner: My oxen and fattened cattle have been butchered, and everything is ready. Come to the wedding banquet'" (Mathew 22:4).

Public Enemies Too

Jesus went the extra mile not only for personal enemies (feeding those who would later tear him down, healing the wound of one who arrested him, forgiving those who crucified him) but also for "public enemies" — those whom most people disliked (healing loved ones of a Roman centurion and Herodian official).

Of all the public enemies Jesus reached out to, the instance that showcases his extreme bravery, tenderness, and patience is his interaction with the demon-possessed man called Legion (see Mark 5:1-19; Luke 8:26-39). In our familiarity with the story, we forget that he was Public Enemy #1 in his locale. He was a terrorist who did not allow anyone to come through his territory (see Matthew 8:28, where he appears to have had an equally scary companion). Avoiding Legion and his screaming (especially during funerals in the graveyard where he lived), chaining him up, and paying for all the chains he broke was undoubtedly a hot topic in this area: more tax money for chains and to pay the men who would chain Legion. It's a wonder that no one "accidentally" killed him. No doubt a lot of energy went into reviling him (as he had probably reviled and insulted many). To say the least, when he was hungry, few were eager to feed him.

But with this public enemy, Jesus goes the extra mile first with mercy. He takes time from his preaching and healing — an entire day or more — to cross the lake and come to help this ultimate "homeless" person of his day. Imagine yourself as a disciple with Jesus in the boat pulling up to the shore. First, what you see is a violent man who is naked. This X-rated spectacle makes you glad you didn't bring your kids along that day. You are also leery of this graveyard by the sea and that this man lives in these caves of the dead. Does he disappear into them at times? As you get closer, you notice his cuts and bruises, for Legion is a "cutter" who mutilates his own flesh at the pleasure of the demon. The noise might upset you by now, for he often shouts and cries, and the manacles of the chains dangling from his arms and legs clank and rattle. If you get close enough, you notice the odor of the dried blood and perhaps an unbathed body. Can you see and hear Legion's agony?

If we put ourselves in the place of the disciples in the boat, we become mesmerized by how Jesus walks up to him, meets his needs, and shows him compassion. How does Legion come to be "clothed and in his right mind" (Mark 5:15, NRSV)? Where do the clothes come from? Do the disciples donate them, or does Jesus miraculously create them? Who helps him dress, avoiding his cuts and bruises? Who takes time to smooth the inevitably tangled, uncut hair and clean his beard? He has no mirror. By the time the townspeople arrive, they find Legion "sitting at Jesus' feet," learning from Jesus just as Mary of Bethany did (Luke 8:35).

Jesus' person and manner draws this formerly crazed man to plead with Jesus not to leave. But Jesus suggests a better idea. He asks this man to do as he does: embrace his enemies. Will he go back to town and preach to the people who chained him up? Jesus tells him, "Return home and tell how much God has done for you" (Luke 8:39). You watch as the now-clean and freed man goes away and tells "all over town" — actually ten towns — how much Jesus has done for him (Luke 8:39; Mark 5:20). Apparently he does a good job because when Jesus returns to this area, people come to him who already believe in him (see Mark 7:31).

Jesus gives Legion not only mercy but also justice. With courage, he frees him from the terrifying demons and releases him from his chains. His "clean bill of health" is signed in the dust cloud of the pigs running into the sea. It convinces him he is finally clean and also gives proof to the only local witnesses (the herdsmen) who could later vouch for his story. Jesus' allowing the demons to go into the pigs as they requested (more compassion?) becomes the necessary proof the former Legion is now clean. There is no longer any reason to mistreat or mistrust him. He can even trust himself.

One time while meditating on this passage, I was struck by these words: "So [Jesus] got into the boat and left" (Luke 8:37). When do the disciples get back in the boat? Do the disciples (of whom I'd imagined myself as one) ever get *out* of the boat? Perhaps they do, but it isn't stated. I saw myself as a disciple who sat in the boat all day, too afraid or disgusted to go ashore. That would have been going one extra mile too far for me. It's not as if Jesus is asking me to jump in the lake, but I could accompany him on shore and work alongside him. Am I willing to do that? Am I willing to get out of the boat, to go the extra mile?

SERVING ENEMIES?

While most of us would pat ourselves on the back for living a life of nonretaliation (turning the other cheek and so on), we might find the idea of expending ourselves for the one who wrongs us (or would if he could) leaving us in the dust. Picture it: When you make a snide comment about me, I don't attack you back (or even think it). I can let your comment stand. Instead I am free to remain available and even vulnerable, to prefer to be injured rather than ever to injure, to not go out of my way to defend myself, to act in the spirit of love by giving more than is asked of me, to try to help the person attacking me, to give to people who have no reason to think I would.[1]

While we find ourselves so often absorbed in me-myself-and-I that we're not paying attention to others, Jesus invites us to allow him to transform us into the kind of people who gladly walk extra miles, grasp and clasp hands about to strike us, grin in the face of epithets, and ask ourselves about the person criticizing us, *What would it look like to love this person?*

A power practice in learning to replace contempt with a focused, clean, and compassionate heart is to serve a difficult person in your life. Maybe you're thinking it's phony to serve someone you dislike. It could be unless you ask God to show you how to serve this difficult person in order to develop a right heart. Also, remember the guideline: "Pray as you can, not as you can't." In this case, serve as you can, not as you can't. Ask God to show you something doable — don't try to be a hero.

Many years ago I knew an older woman who found the pastor annoying. She couldn't stand to listen to his sermons, but she knew she needed to change her attitude. Led by God, she started attending the pastor's weekly Bible study and fixing the coffee and setting up the chairs. I noticed how she appeared to sleep through most of the study, and so I asked if she was tired. As we talked, she revealed to me her problem and the Spirit-suggested solution, saying, "This has helped me see him differently. I find myself praying for him during the study. This was the best thing I could have done."

Her example of going the extra mile for someone she disliked has inspired me to do odd things over the years. One time when my daughter was in grade school, I was very frustrated that she continually forgot to bring home and take back her permission slips. After a not-so-pleasant discussion about this, she left for school and I collapsed in despair. Then I decided to serve her. I went into her room and made her rarely-if-ever-made bed. I ended up having a great time setting up all her My Little Ponies in a circle and thinking what a delightful daughter I had. Another time after a meeting at church, I saw I was parked next to someone I'd found very irritating in the meeting. The ash from a recent wildfire covered all of our cars, so I got a duster from my trunk and gently wiped off his car. The movement was a prayer of sorts — one I was too annoyed to have verbalized — and by the time I was done, I was again able to care about him. Do such little things matter? Yes, because they retrain us (in small ways) to live an eternal kind of life out of the kingdom of God.

EXPERIMENTS IN CONNECTING WITH GOD
(Spiritual Practices to Consider)

To RECEIVE this greatness of spirit from God

Meditation: Read Luke 8:26-39 and Mark 5:1-19 and picture it happening. Where do you see yourself? Write down the feelings you would have had if you had been this person. Jot down anything else about Jesus that comes to you.

Meditation: Read Luke 15:11-32. In whom do you see yourself in this passage? What do you admire most about the Rancher-Father? What do you need the Rancher-Father to say to you today?

Prayer: Thank God for the ways he has gone out of his way for you in the last week.

Prayer: Rephrase Luke 6:27-38, thanking God for being self-giving love: *Thank you that you love your enemies. Thank you that you do good to those who hate you.*

Prayer: Pray the following prayer attributed to Saint Francis of Assisi and thank God for people who have this spirit of Jesus in them:

> Lord, make me an instrument of your peace
> Where there is hatred, let me sow love
> Where there is injury, pardon
> Where there is doubt, faith
> Where there is despair, hope
> Where there is darkness, light
> Where there is sadness, joy
> Divine Master, grant that I may

not so much seek to be consoled as to console,
not so much to be understood as to understand,
not so much to be loved as to love
For it is in giving that we receive.
It is in pardoning that we are pardoned.
It is in dying that we awaken to eternal life.[2]

To BECOME one who offers greatness of spirit to others

Celebration: Ask God to show you a person who needs a little celebration that you could provide.

Fasting: Every time you feel hungry, pray for a "public enemy" that you would like to see turned around.

Fellowship: Whom might you contact who has looked rather dejected lately (e.g., the person who sits in the back at church, the neighbor who rarely waves at you)?

Journal: Ask God to show you who your everyday enemy is — someone you're annoyed with or mildly frustrated with. Let God bring people to your mind. What do you need to say to God about them?

Practicing the presence of God: What breath prayer might you pray to bless each person you pass today at work?

Sacrifice: What might you consider giving to someone else because that person needs it more than you do?

Service and secrecy: Do something for someone you dislike without the person's knowing it and ask God to be with you in it.

Service: Ask God to show you how you might serve a difficult person in your life.

Welcoming the stranger: What "strange" person, perhaps even a public enemy, might you pray for and ask God to show you how you might welcome in some way?

QUESTIONS FOR DISCUSSION AND REFLECTION

1. What does this chapter lead you to want to pray?
2. How do you respond to this view of Jesus as a radical blesser of enemies and even public enemies?
3. What sort of "extra-mile" activity might God be calling you to?
4. Which of the experiments listed do you see yourself trying out this week?

PART 3

JESUS, THE CONFIDENT, PURPOSEFUL SAVIOR

10 Purposeful Intentionality

When Jesus got up every morning, he knew why he was here. Whether he was interacting with fellow carpenter-laborers, walking dusty roads with his disciples, or carrying a cross up a Judean hill, he aimed to reveal who God was through his God-image-bearing life, death, and resurrection (see John 14:9). His earthly visit was part of an exciting cosmic drama in which God makes "himself known by personally approaching human beings and involving himself in their lives."[1]

Jesus didn't come to earth to simply impart a new moral teaching but to reveal the next part of this divine drama—a "mystery hidden for ages in God who created all things" (Ephesians 3:9, NRSV). It's a "grand, epic narrative that runs from the Garden of Eden . . . to the city which is the Bride of the Lamb. It is a love story . . . a dance in which we are invited to join."[2] To Jesus, completing God's work was food that nourished him (see John 4:34; 17:4).

These purposes—to reveal God, to demonstrate how we live interactively with God, and to pass on this love to others in this new kind of life—made it worthwhile to Jesus to be patient with disciples who didn't understand, to be scrutinized closely by those who planned to kill him, and to stand before a Roman governor and speak about truth. Jesus invites us — his body — to abide in him and thereby live this life of mercy and justice, compassion and truth.

JESUS, A PERSON OF MISSION

Jesus was so intentional about his reason for being here that he could not be dissuaded from this task. Even as a young man he willingly upset those he loved by staying behind in Jerusalem because these eternal purposes drew him to talk to people in the temple who had also thought about these purposes. (Did any of the temple teachers live long enough to ask *him* questions twenty years later?)

Jesus' single-mindedness could not be deterred that day or the day he preached his "graduate sermon" back in his hometown of Nazareth (see Luke 4:16-30). There he stated clearly his down-to-earth tasks in the words of a forerunner in the story, Isaiah. Even though Nazarenes were offended by his personalizing Isaiah's mission for himself, Jesus didn't concern himself with being accepted or applauded in speaking. Nor did he go out of his way to be a rabble-rouser. Projecting a certain image was never the point. The point was to share treasured secrets he knew about God. He had no ax to grind or theory to knock down. Jesus was so secure in his identity that he wasn't afraid of upsetting his audience (as I am). That day in Nazareth, attempted murder didn't make him reconsider what he should say. Instead he moved on to Capernaum, where he continued to speak the truth with authority (see Luke 4:32).

When Jesus pressed forward on a mission, *nothing* distracted him. As he headed for the sickbed of Jairus's daughter, I doubt if he heard the mourners and bystanders laughing at him for saying she wasn't dead. He moved forward to do what he came to do — raise her from the dead.

Although many misunderstood him, one person who seemed to get the central pieces of his message (follow me, learn from me, abide in me) was Mary of Bethany, the sister of Martha and Lazarus. She knew "only one thing is needed" and she chose it (Luke 10:41-42). Nothing distracted her from sitting at the feet of Jesus, the normal place of any student of a well-loved teacher. She was so intent on serving him that she later publicly embarrassed herself by anointing Jesus (see John 12:1-8). This "outrageous gesture of anointing Jesus' feet and wiping them with her hair . . . [was] roughly the equivalent, [during] a modern polite dinner party, of a woman hitching up a long skirt to the top of her thighs. You can imagine the onlookers' reaction. Had she no shame?"[3] Who would marry her *now*? Her single-minded devotion to Jesus spurred her to do unthinkable things.

Following Jesus

what do I want? But do I really want it

Interacting with Jesus in this present moment inevitably forces us to examine our intentionality or lack of it. Jesus presses us to answer this question, "What is it you want?" as he did two of his closest friends (and probably everyone else with whom he came into contact).

Put yourself in the scene. James and John, the "Sons of Thunder," and their mother (who could be nicknamed Mama Thunder) come to him, falling before him on their knees and asking him to do *whatever* they request (see Matthew 20:20-28). Instead of advising these three that this grandiose request is rather presumptuous, Jesus asks them that central question: "What is it you want?"

The three state their request: May James and John have honored seats when Jesus comes into his kingdom? (When I have seen myself as one of the disciples, I have first felt indignant that they'd ask for such a thing and then envious that I didn't think of it first. If you see yourself as James or John or Mama Thunder, you might feel high hopes rising inside you; you wouldn't ask if you didn't think there was a chance.)

Instead of answering them directly, Jesus asks them another question: "Can you drink the cup I am going to drink?" Most commentators think that this referred to the "cup of suffering," which could be so, and that they realized this. If they didn't, the young men would connect the appropriate dots in a few days when, in their drowsiness in the garden of Gethsemane, they overhear Jesus ask for a certain cup to pass by him. For now, whatever they think the "cup" is, they are confident they can drink it: "We can," they say.

Of course these three don't know what they're talking about, but Jesus overlooks that and prophesies that they will indeed drink from such a cup. (And they did. James became the first apostle martyred, perhaps within weeks of this scene, and John lived so long that all of his friends were tortured, murdered, or martyred before he was exiled.)

Jesus' two questions in this passage are central questions for any of his followers:

"What is it you want?" (verse 21).

"Can you drink the cup I am going to drink?" (verse 22). (This could also be phrased, "Do you really want to follow me? Is abiding in me worth *anything*?")

If we follow Jesus, answering these two questions over and over becomes a rhythm in our life. One time I was leading a retreat for a church my husband served as a pastor. The group was torn in two over an upcoming decision. Each side was begging my husband to do what they wanted and refusing to speak to those they disagreed with. When he verbalized his thoughts to a few, they found they disagreed with him and stopped speaking to us. On the last morning of the retreat I wanted to cancel my planned talk and give them all a sermon on how to love each other. Instead I delayed and gave the planned talk, closing with a meditation on the passage just discussed. I sent them out on the grounds to ponder the passage, but I planned to call down fire on them when they got back (in love, of course).

Alone and lying on the floor of the meeting room, I found Jesus relentlessly asking me the two questions in the passage. First, "What is it you want?" I wanted these people to love each other and to stop picking on my husband.

Second, "Can you drink the cup I am going to drink?" I had a hunch that cup of suffering and sacrifice was to love people without getting on my high horse and telling them what to do. But that's not what I wanted. I lay there and wept. *I would give them a piece of my mind!* But the figure of Mama Thunder drew my attention, so I read the passage again, wondering, *How much did* she *drink this cup?* I looked up other references about her until I came to one that told me she witnessed the Crucifixion. Putting myself in her place, I knew that as she watched the Crucifixion she, like any mother, would have foreseen in Jesus' suffering the future suffering of her sons. It was as if Jesus said to me, "She drank the cup. Can you?" I couldn't turn down a personal invitation like that. So when the group returned, I finished the retreat with great love, not spouting off as I had wanted to.

Jesus knew what he wanted — to give us a real-life picture of the Father, to show us how to live interactively with God and others in an eternal kind of life — and so he moved forward with purposeful intentionality. Today he invites us into this divine drama and empowers us to join him in this work now.

CULTIVATING SINGLENESS OF HEART

When we get up in the morning, we may have grand ideas of what to do today but do not follow through. That's why Jesus' first question — What is it you want? — is one of the most important questions a follower of Jesus must consider. It's important to answer it not with what you think you're supposed to say or what you think God might want to hear. Take time to let this answer come from the depths of you: What do you *really* want?

Start Where You Are

Most people are unaware of what they really want. They answer this question a certain way — a life with God, to love people more, to grow in Christ — but in reality their actions tell us they want something else, perhaps: to fulfill their self-image of being productive (or fun or responsible or a good pastor or a good mom or . . .); to have others think well of them; to fail because they unconsciously do not think they have a choice or right to want anything else.

Without our realizing it, our soul, which is "almost totally beyond conscious awareness,"[4] is running our life according to our true wants. Our behavior is perfectly designed to try to achieve the goal we truly want. So our behaviors, attitudes, and frequent thoughts are our best clues as to what we really want: the behaviors on which we spend most of our time and effort every day; the thoughts to which our minds drift; the things on which we spend our money; the things we find ourselves complaining about. When we review our calendar, checkbook entries, in-between thoughts, and frequent conversations with people we trust, we find that most of our time and energy go into achieving and acquiring (so we can feel fulfilled or be looked up to), trying to have good feelings, or controlling the people around us. We don't discern these things easily, so it's wise to ask God to reveal to us in prayer what our real wants are. Then we have a place to start because we know what truly governs our life.

For several years, doing our income tax return became a spiritual revelation to me. One year I couldn't believe how much money I had spent on books. Although these books were excellent, I wondered if the people I lived with ever saw my face. Was I loving my in-house neighbors as myself? Even more revealing was to review the things about which I complained to my husband. What topics has he heard me grumble about more than once? This revealed to me that what I really wanted was to get the credit I thought I deserved and stop the world from being so rude, at least to me. As I pondered letting those wants go, I saw I'd be more able to bless my husband (which is what I really want).

Ask God to Show You Where You Want to Go

Such brutal honesty drives us to this question: What do I *want* to want? When I transfer to the next world (die), how do I hope I will have benefited the people aiound me? What do I hope I will have accomplished? Instead of doing routine things that good people do, have we investigated what breaks our heart and the heart of God?[5] There are some needs, deficiencies, and pain-filled dilemmas on this planet that call out to each of us and for which we need courage to risk working for. God draws us to some good thing that bears his image, characterizes the divine drama, and so furthers his purposes. This thing that breaks our heart is the place where God's pain and our pain intersect, where God's mystery and our purpose meet. To think about what this calling (or purpose) might be requires investigation. We ask ourselves, *If I were to explore that good thing God wants done, what would be my first step?*

Am I Willing?

In order to do what we truly want to do, we have to address Jesus' second question: Can I drink the cup (of sacrifice) that Jesus drank? To do so would mean giving up normal self-focused desires — reputation, having my way, being entertained.

It's even more difficult to become willing to give up self*less* desires and activities that distract us from what we want to want. Good things can become "stumbling blocks" or weights that so easily encumber us (Matthew 18:7-9, NRSV; see Hebrews 12:1). We may need to set aside important things (being respected, a higher income, extended leisure time) to know God better and follow Jesus into a radical life. Most of our distractions are so good (family, church, health, work) that it doesn't occur to us that our intense focus on them causes us to miss out on union with God. The enormous amount of attention we pay to these important things may leave us used up. Not everything deserves the intensity of focus and extended time and energy we spend on it.

Jesus' second question invites us to consider if we want what we want *enough* to give up these other good things. For example, in order to have time to do what I really want to do — spend time with

God, do the work of writing and speaking and spiritual direction, and hang out with family (board-game playing, current events discussions, and just plain "porch sitting") — I have simplified the way I provide meals for my family. When my kids were small, I shopped for groceries only once a month. It took planning, but it was worth it. Eventually I stopped cooking every night and cooked just a few times a week. On Wednesday, we ate the same thing as Monday and so on. Once my kids went off to college, I cooked only once a week and my husband and I enjoyed the same meal every night. I've been told by people that they could never do this. Neither could I until I wanted something else more. Variety in eating just isn't as important to me as those three items I named. Such "sacrifices" simplify life immensely. Instead of living in confusion and distraction, we live with peace and purposeful intentionality.

Jesus pictured this singleness of heart with a guy who was digging in a field — probably working hard and minding his own business — when he found a treasure buried there. Don't you imagine that after he recovered from this shock he looked around to make sure no one noticed his hesitation and then covered up the treasure? Then *with joy* he sold everything — the house, the farm, the horses, even the savings bonds his grandfather gave him. With nothing else to his name, he presented the money to purchase the field, actually the treasure. This is something you and I can do — divest ourselves of everything else we thought we wanted because we have found the treasure we truly *want*.

The treasure finder took a risk, which is also part of our cup of sacrifice. Am I willing to do what I sense I'm being called to do even if it looks foolish to others? Someone probably thought the treasure wasn't worth what he sacrificed, but he knew it was. Jesus risked being misunderstood and being persecuted many days of his life. Mary of Bethany risked social rejection. James risked his life and was slain. John risked his and lived through the glory (and the persecution) of the early church. To follow Jesus single-mindedly requires risk, but it's a risk based on faith in God. As we connect with God, we trust God in that soul-friend relationship to walk with us through this calling.

Disciplines for Singleness of Heart

Hardworking, purposeful people easily get distracted and lose their focus when they don't regularly pause to connect with God and let God reinvite them to do the work of the kingdom. Without solitude, they get sidetracked by people's demands and their own ambition until their body breaks down. Solitude creates space for servants of God to practice reflection, which is what this chapter is about. We need to quietly reflect on the questions presented here. In reflection, we hear our real thoughts (what we *really* want). Then we can confess them and ask God to show us our next steps.

The discipline of service also reminds us of whose we are and what we're here for. When I speak on weekends, I receive more positive reinforcement than is good for me. Getting up early on Monday mornings, pulling on old clothes that will get stained with bleach, and driving to the Samaritan Center reminds me of who I really am: a simple follower of Jesus who is privileged to wash other people's underwear.

Frugality eliminates distractions. It helps us ask, *What can I give away?* instead of, *What can I buy?* To practice frugality, one of my students chose to give away one piece of clothing each time he bought a new one—even workout clothes of which he had a drawerfull. Another promised his wife he would limit himself to buying one item whenever he went into his favorite ninety-nine-cents store. A friend practiced frugality by fasting from shopping during Lent. For forty days, she shopped only when her family needed something, and she bought nothing for herself. Her evaluation: "Life was so much better, less hectic."

Solitude, reflection, service, frugality, and other disciplines remind us of what it looks like to follow Jesus. As they form a steady rhythm in our lives, we become free to do what we really want to do.

Keep in mind: What Father, Son, and Spirit *want* is *you* — to bring you and the rest of the planet into their marvelous kingdom, where you join them in their circle of love, joy, and peace. You can be part of that kingdom — living in the Trinitarian presence — by passionately pursuing what it means to be a disciple of Jesus. Asking you the question, What is it you want? is one way God woos you into eternal life right now. As you struggle to discern the answer to the question, it's wise to gaze at the purposeful, focused life of Jesus that you are invited to share.

EXPERIMENTS IN CONNECTING WITH GOD
(Spiritual Practices to Consider)

To ABSORB this purposeful intentionality from God

Meditation: Read Matthew 20:20-28 and picture the scene. Whom does God invite you to become in this passage? Write down the feelings you would have had if you had been this person. Jot down anything else about Jesus that comes to you.

Solitude: Choose one: Put a personal retreat on your calendar and do it; or take a ten-minute nap in your car tomorrow on your lunch break; or take a walk to a new place. Or if you're a mother of young children, tell your kids that when Mom's in the bathroom, she's having her "time-out" and no one must talk to her. Then take your time-out at least twice a day.

To BECOME a purposefully intentional disciple of Jesus

Fasting: Go without food for a period of time. Then journal on these two questions: What is it you want? Are you willing to follow Jesus?

Frugality: Reflect on what possessions or activities eat up your time or energy. What are you willing to get rid of?

Frugality: How are you willing to limit your time spent in stores? To limit your purchases?

Prayer: Ask God to help you be more single-minded and to show you your next step.

Reflection and confession (perhaps journaling): Examine the question, What is it you want? Allow time to adequately reflect on it. Keep coming back to it for at least a week. Don't be afraid to be ruthlessly honest with God and yourself: to be noticed, to have others look up to you, to be the best___. Say it all.

Reflection: Write down all the things you do in one week or one day. Set this before God and ask God to help you simplify or set aside the tasks that are less important to what you really want.

Reflection: Ponder the idea of coping with plenty ("I know how to do without, and I know how to cope with plenty," Philippians 4:12[6]). How do you cope with plenty when you receive a raise? When you sit at a Thanksgiving holiday meal?

Sacrifice: Give up a convenience, self-indulgence, or sentimentality that eats up your time. What does this free you to do or be?

Service: Examine all the ways in which you serve. Which ones point most clearly to the things that break your heart and the heart of God? What are you doing just because no one else will do it?

Solitude and Reflection: Take a walk and ponder the best moments of your life. When do timeless moments occur (usually in creativity, worship, or substantive fellowship)? What are you doing to make room for more of those moments to happen? Don't ask yourself these questions until you have been quiet for a while, your breathing has slowed, and your shoulders are relaxed.

Study: Look through a concordance and notice the instances in which "get up" occurs in the Gospels and Acts. Do you identify with any of these people told to "get up"? What else do you notice about these instances? Do you need to "get up"? If so, how?

QUESTIONS FOR DISCUSSION AND REFLECTION

1. What do you want people to remember most about you?
2. What do you really want?
3. What are some of your greatest distractions?
4. How might you practice solitude or frugality this week?
5. Which of the experiments listed do you see yourself trying out this week?

❧

CS Lewis quote -
finding Jesus
the world

11   No Fear

What would you say is the most frequent command in the Bible? The following answer by N. T. Wright surprised me:

 What instruction, what order, is given, again and again, by God, by angels, by Jesus, by prophets and apostles? What do you think—"Be good"? "Be holy"? Or, negatively, "Don't sin"? "Don't be immoral"? No. The most frequent command in the Bible is: *"Don't be afraid." "Fear not."*[1]

This idea jarred me. Yet just a few minutes of study showed me that this command is a repeated melody in the symphony of Scripture: God said it to Abraham, Moses, Joshua; an angel said these words to Mary and Zechariah; Jesus said them to the mother of a dead child (Jairus's wife—had she just burst into tears?). Jesus told the disciples not to be afraid of the power they saw in a miraculous catch of fish, of the earth's terrifying elements, of men who would beat and persecute them, of him when he walked on water, of him when they saw him in radiance talking with Moses and Elijah (who *were*, after all, deceased), of him in his post-resurrection body (see Luke 5:10;

Matthew 8:26; 10:26; 14:27; 17:7; 28:10).

Furthermore, this command fits with that major biblical theme: trusting God. The Bible's subtitle could be *Holy Bible: Trust Me!* "Don't be afraid" is "Trust me!" turned inside-out. Both are the bass notes underneath, "The Lord *really* is my shepherd. I *really* do have everything I need." If I'm not afraid, I can lie down in the green pasture as this sheep did because I have nothing to fear: no dangers, no shortage of food.

"Don't be afraid" speaks to the anxiety that drives much of our waywardness. When we're afraid, we often use anger to protect ourselves. In fear, we attempt to manage and control those we love and don't love, alienating them all and proving we don't trust God. Out of fear, we deceive others to get our needs met because we don't trust God to meet our needs.

We may be afraid of failure but also of success; rejection but also of intimacy; looking unattractive but also of looking too attractive; how others are looking at me or that no one notices me; disappointing authority figures or being that disappointing figure myself. We fear that we somehow won't have what we need or the relationships we need. We're afraid that we'll get into a difficult situation and God won't show up in time. We're afraid that we'll be found out — others will discover I'm not the person they think I am. These fears move us to violate our conscience so that to do wrong seems like the only way to survive a troubled marriage or cutthroat workplace.

ENTER JESUS

Our familiarity with Jesus' behavior numbs the appropriate amazement we should have of his bravery, guts, nerve, daring, and confidence. Consider his constant courage.

Living with death threats. From the moment the Nazarene crowd attempted to push Jesus off the cliff, Jesus lived in constant danger (see Matthew 21:46; John 7:1; 11:57). Do we know what this is like? Martin Luther King Jr.'s biographer described the wear and tear daily death threats had on King. This brave man whose home was bombed and who repeatedly faced mobs and armed men got so "toward the end of his life he was able to relax only when surrounded by friends in rooms without windows."[2] I'm sure I could not have been as fearless as Dr. King, which makes Jesus beyond believable.

When Jesus' opponents picked up stones to kill him (much like a lynch mob), he simply talked to them (see John 10:31-39). Later in that confrontation and at another time when they moved to stone him, he simply slipped away (see John 8:59; 10:39). After Jesus raised Lazarus from the dead, the Pharisees renewed their plots to kill him, but instead of hiding, Jesus led the way on his final trip to Jerusalem, warning the terrified disciples that he would be betrayed, ridiculed, beaten, killed, and rise again (see Mark 10:32-34). Instead of sneaking into town, Jesus openly rode into Jerusalem with great fanfare. That's an odd thing for a man to do whose picture was on the Most Wanted List (see John 12:12-19).

Earlier, when the temple police came to arrest Jesus, he sent them away, telling them it wasn't time yet. *They actually went away,* much to the confusion of the chief priests and Pharisees. Their explanation was, "No one ever spoke the way this man does" (John 7:46; see also 32-34,45-49).

Being arrested. When the actual arrest took place, the scene was backward. *Jesus* confronted the *mob* twice by saying, "Who is it you want?" (John 18:4,7). Nor was he quick to be arrested — what with the crowd falling backward and his pausing to heal someone (see John 18:6; Luke 22:51). He could have walked through this crowd untouched as he did in Nazareth, but instead he courageously moved forward to his "glory" (see John 7:39).

Being beaten. Jesus continued fearlessly with no cowering or shrinking back. In the face of insults, taunts, and beatings, no complaint or murmur or indignant reproach or even cry of pain is recorded. This humble courage is so different from what we know.

The daring heroes of movies are usually arrogant. They yell a lot. You have to get out of their way or be trampled. Not so with Jesus. He was "not defenseless, but undefending, not vanquished, but uncontending, not helpless, but majestic in voluntary self-submission for the highest purpose of love."[3]

PRINCE OF PEACE

One of Jesus' "Don't be afraid" quotations is prefaced by, "Peace I leave with you; my peace I give you. I do not give to you as the world gives. Do not let your hearts be troubled and do not be afraid" (John 14:27). He said this to the grieving disciples when they were afraid of the future filled with harsh, murderous people. "Peace be with you" was his greeting from the resurrected body whether he was making a surprise appearance or sending them forth (see Luke 24:36; John 20:19,21,26).

But Jesus' most remembered words of peace are, "Peace, be still" as he calmed the storm. One time when I led a group in meditating on this passage, a young woman insisted she would not have been afraid because, after all, Jesus was in the boat. I'm astounded by her trust, but I think it stems from her knowing the end of the story. I would have been afraid because I've known people who have drowned while boating in *calm* water. I was tossed overboard from a raft in rapids on a relatively small river and had to be pulled back in by a guide. The disciples' fear is real to me.

As I ponder this passage, I imagine that the disciples lunge forward, losing their balance as the boat keeps shifting under them. They hold on to the sides or anything else they can grab. They no doubt slip and fall and are probably bleeding, but they don't notice because they are already wet. The wind sweeps back their hair and whips their soaked clothes around them until they are shivering. Some try to manage the sail, while others bail water. Tired and out of breath, they feel fear filling their gut.

Some of them wake up the peacefully sleeping Jesus to say, "Teacher, don't you care if we drown?" (Mark 4:38). They want to know if he is concerned for them and maybe if he is smart and powerful enough to do something. You can easily imagine their panicked faces as they ask this. But it is most difficult to imagine — but please try — the calm face of Jesus, who actually talks *to* the wind and talks *to* the sea — two entities you and I have never had conversation with (see Mark 4:35-41). This is Jesus unafraid — at home with nature, at home with caring for his disciples. When you've seen Jesus you've seen God, and this tells us God can be trusted.

In the exquisite Rembrandt painting *The Storm on the Sea of Galilee*,[4] our eyes are drawn first to the left, where bright yellow light shines on the sail as the disciples tug at it and the sea invades the boat. But after taking all this in, our eyes slowly move to another light in the stern of the boat, where a few people sit huddled peacefully in the dark, two of them fixing their gaze on the lit face of Jesus (on the right).

I've lived too much of my life in the chaotic left side of the picture, tugging at the sails and trying to manage the wind and the waves myself. Perhaps you have battled storms too. Jesus invites us to move to the stern, where he sits in peace, and to join the ones gazing at him.

PICTURES OF PEACE

Part of what Jesus routinely did, then, was to help people move from a place of fear to a place of trust — the journey each of us takes every day: Will I trust Jesus today with this task that's too big for me, this rancorous relationship, this physical body that no longer does what it used to do?

As we make this journey of transformation into Christlikeness, we let go of fear and learn to trust Jesus today, even if only for ten minutes at a time. One of the best ways to connect with God and find both courage and peace is to cultivate pictures in the mind such as the one just described. What happened on the Sea of Galilee was not fantasy. The reality of Jesus and his power overcame the force of the wind and quieted it. Within us each day, Jesus can overpower our fear and chaos and quiet us with peace. We need to have a picture of it firmly planted in our mind and his words "Peace, be still" on our lips.

While the picture of Jesus calming the sea is powerful, another scene in Jesus' life fits my everyday circumstances even better. In this down-to-earth picture of Jesus' serenity, he acts out Psalm 23:5: sitting across the table from his enemies but in complete peace as the Anointed One. Even in the presence of his enemies, he is not intimidated by *anyone* (as I am).

The table is situated in the home of the leader of the Pharisees, where Jesus is a guest (see Luke 14:1-6). It is the Sabbath and "he was being carefully watched." The word for "watched" is the word used for "'sinister espionage.' Jesus was under scrutiny."[5] Noticing the man with crippling swelling in his joints (dropsy), Jesus challenges the watchers: "Is it lawful to heal on the Sabbath or not?" His adversaries are silent, so Jesus takes hold of the man, heals him, and sends him away from the controversy.

Jesus' calmness both puzzles and fascinates me. First, think about how you behave under negative scrutiny. Take yourself back to high school and imagine your geometry teacher standing over you as you take a test, the same teacher who called you "stupid" the day before. Feeling panicky and demoralized, you need courage and serenity to provide you with the necessary clearheaded thinking to answer the test questions. Apparently Jesus had these. We can also assume Jesus possessed a "right heart" (focused, clean, and compassionate) toward these questioners based on how those involved in healing ministry inform us of the necessity of having one's heart free of resentment and full of trust in God to be a useful pipeline of God's healing power.[6] "He did His Work of power and love unrestrained by their evil thoughts."[7] Compare this scene with the one in which the disciples could not cast out a demon — which they had done easily before. Had the scribes unnerved them or made them angry? (See Mark 9:14-18; Luke 9:1-6.)

After healing the man with dropsy, Jesus questions his opponents further, but they have nothing to say again. Jesus had that pure and weighty presence that leaves opponents speechless. A steel gut alone would not have been free of resentment. An overflow of compassion alone would not have confronted his opponents. Jesus' knowledge of who he was and what he came for gave him a courageous, compassionate, serene presence in the face of tormentors. They "could watch him all they liked, but the power both of his healings and of his explanations was too strong for them."[8]

As I meditated on this passage once, I found myself puzzled about why Jesus would go to eat at a Pharisee's home in the first place. Come on — these difficult people weren't going to listen to him! He could have found this suffering man elsewhere. This suggestion helped me: "Jesus never refused any man's invitation of hospitality. To the end, He never abandoned hope of men. To hope to change them, or even to appeal to them — He would never let a chance go. He would not refuse even an enemy's invitation. We will never make our enemies our friends if we refuse to meet them and to talk with them."[9] This possibility put Jesus in a new light for me. It meant that Jesus didn't go there and simply endure the stress of it all. I tend to do this; *Just get through this*, I tell myself. This does not help. It forces on me a victim identity and throws me into self-pity: *Why do I have to go through this?* Instead of acting with gritty endurance or silent suffering, Jesus came full of hope, looking for the one or two who would eventually believe. Courage grows by replacing cynicism with hope and self-pity with trust. Seeing Jesus this way, I suddenly felt brave and wanted to be a disciple alongside Jesus in the home of our enemies. I could sit there full of hope, not intimidated but content, peaceful, and even a little joyful. Such is life in the kingdom of God.

EXPERIMENTS IN CONNECTING WITH GOD
(Spiritual Practices to Consider)

To ABSORB this fearless courage of God

Celebration: Read aloud Psalm 23 and after each main phrase, add this one: "no matter what." Try it a second time, saying "no matter what" with fierce determination. Repeat this until you mean it.

Confession: Admit your fears to God to release their power over you. Try to get at your core issues with these questions: What drives you to feel you have to stretch or change the truth? What drives you to speak harshly?

Meditation: Read Mark 4:35-41 and picture it happening (again, even if you did so earlier). Write down the feelings you would have had if you had been in this boat. Jot down anything else about Jesus that comes to you.

Meditation: Imagine Jesus interceding for you (see Romans 8:34) regarding the fears that rule you at this moment. Consider that this is happening at this moment. Ask Jesus to pray specifically about this protection according to your needs and fears. If you wish, hear Jesus pray, "Holy Father, protect them by the power of your name — the name you gave me — so that they may be one as we are one. . . . My prayer is not that you take them out of the world but that you protect them from the evil one" (John 17:11,15).

Meditation: View a copy of Rembrandt's *Storm on the Sea of Galilee*.[10] Where are you in this painting? Where do you live most of your life? If you live in the chaos, can you picture yourself moving from the place of chaos (on the left) to the place of peace in front of Jesus (on the right)?

Prayer: Offer the prayer "The Breastplate of St. Patrick"[11] for a week slowly. Taste it and let the images fill you. Consider memorizing at least the part that begins, "Christ before me . . ."

Study: Read Psalm 23 every day for a week and study the pictures presented there with the help of a commentary. Can you see yourself sitting courageously across the table from your enemy (see verse 5)? Can you see goodness and mercy becoming a natural result just because you're around (see verse 6)? Then memorize it. Finally, pray it as much as you can in your everyday life—in line at stores, while washing your hands, while heating a drink in the microwave.

Worship: Admire God, who delights in using power for good, using Psalm 27 or Psalm 91.

To BECOME one who experiences this fearless courage of God

Fellowship: Talk to a few friends about fears. What do they think most people are afraid of—especially people who do the kind of work you do? Be courageous—ask them if they have any guesses about what you might be afraid of or if they are willing to admit their own fears. Then take these to God in prayer.

Prayer: Offer the prayer in Ephesians 3:16-21 in which power is highlighted three times. Ask God for power in the same three ways: (1) to strengthen you with power through the Spirit in your inner being; (2) to give you power to grasp how wide and long and high and deep is the love of Christ; (3) to help you acknowledge that because God's power works in us, God is able to do immeasurably more than all we ask or imagine.

Prayer: Consider moments when you feel mistreated and when you might pray Psalm 27:3. Begin by picturing yourself with rows of soldiers in a semicircle around you ("Though an army besiege me"). They're all thinking how dumb you are, yet "my heart will not fear" (not imagining the worst, asking Jesus for ideas about what to do, praying for the redemption and restoration of difficult people, praying to keep moving forward, not letting my thoughts become frozen in fear). "Even then will I be confident" (that God is *with me* no matter what, that God *will meet my needs* no matter what).

Prayer: Pray Psalm 27 or 91 but insert the details of your fears and the appropriate people's names. For example, fill in these blanks of 27:3 (NRSV): "Though ____ encamp against me, my heart shall not fear; though ____ rise up against me, yet I will be confident." You may want to fill in those blanks not with a person's name but with feelings or categories of people: "being overlooked" or "scary surprises" or "arrogant people" or "people who try to thwart me."

Reflection: Journal about someone who scares you. Why does this person scare you?

Sacrifice: Give up something you know you need (bus fare, your lunch) in order to make way for God to provide in miraculous ways, thus increasing your trust.

QUESTIONS FOR DISCUSSION AND REFLECTION

1. Of what you read in this chapter, what did you need to hear most? Why?
2. Which of the fears listed on page 148 are the most common ones for people in your work or family situation?
3. Which situation from Jesus' life would have been most scary to you: living with death threats, being arrested, being beaten, sitting with your opponents, other? What do you admire most about Jesus?
4. What does this chapter lead you to want to pray?
5. Which of the experiments listed do you see yourself trying out this week?

❧

Gary -
Hank on the Ranch

12   Exceptional Teacher

Everyone is a teacher. You are a teacher if anyone has ever learned anything from you. Standing in front of a group in the role of a teacher is not the only way to teach, and sometimes it's not the best way. Although Jesus taught that way, he spent even more time teaching by interacting with people in on-the-spot situations. Every day presented a real-life case study: How would he feed thousands of hungry people? Would he pay the temple tax? How would he respond to his family's rejection? Teaching involves delivering content, but it also means letting people watch how you live and ask you questions about why you do what you do.

Since we're all teachers, it's wise to learn from Jesus how to be practical, clear-thinking, adventurous ones. As Jesus interacted with people, he gave them plenty of latitude, asked questions that made them think, and presented truth in creative ways that woke them up. His teaching possessed an authority and authenticity that amazed people. He had a way of driving truth all the way home to the depths of the soul. He was the kind of teacher that any disadvantaged student could learn from and any careful thinker could be puzzled by. His magnetic style and content draw us to become his students for the rest of our lives.

JESUS' WAY WITH PEOPLE

As a relational person, Jesus' primary way of teaching was to invest in people. "Being with" was his intimate style of teaching. He didn't set up a traveling one-man show, but his team interacted deeply in the lives of people.

Doing things together in everyday life was important because his goal was to train people to *follow* him. As he and the disciples ate together and traveled together, experienced hunger and exhaustion together, he taught them how to live well: to *love* and *serve* God in everything they did. Like today's youth workers, he knew that one week of Christian summer camp is worth more than a year of meetings.

Following Jesus was simple and exciting because Jesus asked others to do only what they first saw him do (see Luke 9:1-6; 10:1-22). As his example drew people into the learning process, he built more than head knowledge. He created understanding and spiritual momentum, which would become so important for his disciples' souls and so vital for the church's beginnings.[1] Life in the kingdom, he knew, would be caught as much as taught.

Because Jesus invested in people, he interacted with individuals according to their needs, enlarging their faith in the precise way they needed rather than using a canned, one-size-fits-all approach. For example, he used speech (indeed lengthy conversation) with the wayward and somewhat reluctant Samaritan woman but silence and terse phrases with the confident Syrophoenician woman. The latter woman's unexpected but somewhat developed faith ("Son of David!") needed only to be pointed in the right direction in order to express an amazing grasp of God's abundant grace. (She understood that even crumbs from Jesus' table could work miracles.) Jesus used different teaching styles to develop the faith of these two quasi-pagan women (see John 4:4-29; Mark 7:24-30). To Jesus, each woman was an individual whose needs cried out to him; they were not projects to be convinced, conquered, and checked off. Even now Jesus does this with us. Depending on the issue and our faith development concerning that issue, Jesus sometimes draws us into lengthy conversation with himself or with others. At other times, he offers difficult flashes of truth in the midst of what appears to be silence.

Teaching with Latitude

Jesus gave his disciples a shocking amount of room for error. With just a little preparation (no seminary), he sent out the seventy-two disciples to heal and to announce that the kingdom of God was near (see Luke 10:9). What an adventure — even the demons submitted to them! (The disciples would not always be so successful. See Mark 9:17-19,28-29.)

To send his followers out on their own was to give them breathing space to make mistakes. In fact, he often gave them enough rope to (hopefully) save themselves or let him save them. Notice especially the long leash Jesus gives Peter — twice! Peter is often derided for sinking when he tries to walk on water, but isn't it amazing that he takes even one step (see Matthew 14:28-33)? What is Peter thinking when he asks to join Jesus out there? What is Jesus thinking to let him? After Peter's short success and failure, he wisely calls out to Jesus, who is within arm's reach as a good teacher would be. When I meditate on this passage, I am never Peter. I am always a sensible disciple clutching the other side of the boat, thinking Peter is nuts. But when Jesus and Peter come safely back into the boat, I find myself envying Peter for his nerve. *Why didn't I try it?* I scold myself. I've also marveled at Jesus for letting Peter try. I've had to learn that a good teacher says, "Try something wild. I'll catch you."

Jesus also gives Peter leeway when Peter boasts that he is ready to go to prison and die with Jesus. Instead of being impressed by this sacrificial devotion, Jesus enlightens Peter that he will instead deny him. In the meantime, Jesus is praying that Peter's faith doesn't fail (see Luke 22:32). Wouldn't a respectable teacher pray that Peter wouldn't deny him at all? But Jesus gives Peter latitude to make mistakes.

As a soul-forming teacher, Jesus focuses his prayer on Peter's developing an abiding, enduring faith in spite of, in the middle of, and even because of his mistake. He's more anxious for Peter to *learn something* in soul school than for Peter to get A's. Jesus prays that Peter's faith won't fail because when we err as Peter did, our faith is likely to fail. We might get inordinately discouraged, but this is usually because our faith is not in God but in *our own* faith — in our ability to be faithful. But if we can freely admit our mistakes and choose to trust the adequacy of God when we fail, our faith grows and we can strengthen others.

Watching how Jesus gave Peter this long leash helped me when our teenage daughter left home for a life of "couch surfing" (sleeping on the couches of different friends every night). At first we prayed, of course, that she would come home. After months of these prayers, I gradually saw that her trek was somehow necessary to her development. She was trying to figure out who she was apart from her parents, and I had to give her room to do some scary things just as Jesus gave Peter room. So besides praying for her safety, I prayed that *her faith would not fail* in this journey. As she saw that we no longer tried to get her to come home and that our trust in her was growing (well . . . trust in God and her), she accepted our invitation to come home once a week for "family dinner." Our support group leaders informed us that this behavior was unheard of for a runaway teen. It was such a treasure for us, of course, giving us ringside seats from which we watched her make better decisions over the next year. What appeared to be her failure taught her a great deal about being the wise and empathetic young woman she is today.

Most of us learn best from failure, which Jesus of course knows. So he tells Peter beforehand, "And when you have turned back, strengthen your brothers." In this way, Jesus laid out Peter's "next steps" after the failure: Don't give up; let God redeem the failure by strengthening others. A good teacher helps you use your failures for good.

Making People Think

Ever the conversational, interactive teacher, Jesus asked questions frequently, even answering questions with questions (see Mark 10:17-18; Luke 20:22-24). But Jesus' purpose in asking questions was not to outsmart people. It was to help them follow truth logically and clearly. Jesus did not aim "to win battles, but to achieve insight and understanding in his hearers. . . . [He used questions] to develop a teaching about the nature of God, which was always his main concern."[2]

Jesus posed questions most frequently to prod people to *think about what they believed about him as God*. For example, he asked the disciples, "Who do people say the Son of Man is?" and then more personally, "Who do *you* say I am?" (Matthew 16:13,15, italics added). Jesus asked two blind men who wanted to be healed if they really thought he could do it (see Matthew 9:28). That's an important question: Do we really believe God is *able* to do what we just spent hours asking God to do?

Jesus asked his followers to *think about what they said*. For example, when Philip said, "Show us the Father," hadn't Philip seen the Father for the last three years (John 14:8-9)? In the midst of Jesus' trying to get Peter to think about his claim that he would lay down his life for Jesus, Jesus repeated back Peter's exact words: "Will you *really* lay down your life for me?" (John 13:37-38, italics added). Such challenging and penetrating questions search a person's will and help them see their true intentions.

Questions allowed Jesus to urge people to *think about what they wanted*, so he asked, "What do you want me to do for you?" of all sorts of inquirers: the blind seeking his help and the proud seeking chief seats in the kingdom (Matthew 20:32; Mark 10:36,51; Luke 18:41). When two of Jesus' soon-to-be disciples followed him, he turned around and asked them, "What do you want?" You can imagine these two guys stammering and fumbling around at being noticed and questioned by the new teacher in town. So they ask him, "Rabbi, where are you staying?" which seems to be their way of saying, "Can we hang out with you?" (John 1:37-38). I imagine Jesus grinned as he answered, "Come and you will see."

Jesus used questions to *probe people's motives*. He knew what people were thinking, but he wanted *them* to discover what they thought and why they thought it (see Mark 2:8). So he asked the man who had been lame for thirty-eight years if he *wanted* to get well (see John 5:6). Instead of answering the rich young ruler's earnest question about what he needed to do to be saved, Jesus replied with a question about his motives: "Why do you call me good?" (Mark 10:17-18). Jesus was leading the young man on a journey of self-discovery of his true motives and finding a vision of the world much greater than he had imagined.

Asking questions trained his followers to understand that life with the Holy One was interactive. This is still true today. We need to get our perspective clear that the Trinity — Father, Son, and Holy Spirit — engages us in conversation and is eager to hear our questions and to ask us questions. As a spiritual director, I love asking directees, "What question is God asking you these days?" and, "What questions are you asking God?" If we're listening to our life, we'll hear God asking us questions such as, "Am I enough?" (God's basic question to Abraham in asking him to offer up Isaac). When God asks us questions, we need to be as honest as Peter was: No, he didn't *agape* Jesus, but he did *phileo* Jesus (see John 21:15-17; selfless love versus friendship love). God asks us these questions to help us see what is within us, so healing and growth can take its next step. Like Peter, we may eventually realize Jesus' goal for us: "Though you have not seen him, you [*agape*] him" (1 Peter 1:8).

Presenting Truth Clearly

As an expert in making truth plain and relevant, Jesus started where people were. In the Sermon on the Mount, he approached many topics by saying, "You have heard that it was said . . ." He began with the prevailing myths of the day, then was quick to turn those myths around: Killing people with your hands is wrong, but killing them in your hearts is also deadly (Matthew 5:21-22, author's paraphrase). Each of those turnarounds focused on helping people embrace the tender kingdom heart. Here are some of his favorite methods of making truth clear — methods we can copy.

Case study. One of Jesus' favorite opening phrases was, "Suppose one of you . . ." (Matthew 12:11, NRSV; Luke 11:5; 14:28; 15:4; 17:7). Then he created the dilemma: Your sheep falls into a pit on the Sabbath; you don't have enough food for an unexpected guest; you want to build a tower. He was inviting them: Put yourself in this person's place. What would you do? What ideas or values govern what you do?

Parables. When Jesus' actions stymied people, he often explained those actions with parables. The parable of the doctor going to the sick instead of the healthy explained why Jesus associated with tax collectors. The parable of the wicked tenants explained why Jesus cleansed the temple. The stories of the lost sheep, coin, and sons explained why he welcomed sinners[3] (Matthew 9:10-12; 21:12-16,33-41; Luke 15:1-32).

When truths particularly stymied people, he used parables as "tools to break open the prevailing worldview and replace it with one that was closely related but significantly adjusted at every point. . . . This is how stories work. They invite listeners into a new world, and encourage them to make that new world their own."[4]

Everyday objects. One of Jesus' most fascinating teaching habits was to pick up whatever was within arm's reach and show how it resembled the kingdom of God. He took whatever was at hand — a vine, tree, seed, plow, yoke, coin — and did this. One time when the disciples argued, he took a child in his arms and declared, "Unless you change and become like little children . . ." (Matthew 18:1-6).

Look at what is within arm's reach of you as you read this book—a glass of water, a chair, a shoe. Consider that Jesus was such an insightful teacher that if he were sitting next to you, he could pick up any of those items and explain how the kingdom of God was just like that item. He would so astound you with the depth of insight that you'd call up a friend and say, "Take off your shoe and look at it. Now see, the kingdom of God is like your shoe because . . ."

Comparisons. Rooted in creation and the concreteness of life, Jesus used metaphors and similes to link commonplace things and activities with ideas he was leading them to understand: "You now fish for fish, but I will make you fishers of *people*" (Mark 1:16-17, author's paraphrase). He was forever breaking bread (the feeding of the five thousand and four thousand, the Last Supper, the house in Emmaus) so that the breaking of his own body made sense. Even now we long to see that metaphor for his body—the broken bread—lifted up in celebration of Communion.

Puzzling statements. Jesus frequently offered statements his hearers did not understand *then.* When he said to Martha at her brother's death, "Your brother will rise again," she probably had little idea of what he meant. But in time, she no doubt understood. College professor Seth Wilson explained Jesus' method: "Jesus liked to give enigmatical statements such as this to cause His hearers to ponder and study for their real meaning. . . . A good teacher does not work everything out for the pupil but gives just enough help to stimulate the utmost intellectual effort. [Jesus] sought to draw out and enlarge the faith of those whom He would help."[5] Perhaps you have wished certain teachers would explain some of the odd things they say. Actually it's helpful to let it lodge like a pebble in your shoe so that it bothers you and you slowly discover its truth. Truth is more meaningful and easily remembered when we discover it ourselves.

Why did Jesus use all these devices? To bring clarity, but also to shock people out of their complacency. Some of his parables were mildly horrifying to wake his listeners up to the truth: much-looked-up-to religious leaders leaving a man to die on the Jericho road; someone forgiven a debt of thousands but not forgiving a debt of pennies; a shepherd abandoning an investment of ninety-nine sheep; a cheater getting by because he built relationships with people! Speaking of such parables, Elton Trueblood commented, "Christ seems to employ exactly that amount of shock which is necessary to make people break through their deeply ingrained obtuseness."[6]

Humor. To further penetrate their inability to understand, Jesus laced these devices with humor as an instrument of grace — to empower them to absorb what they could not otherwise grasp. "Christ used deliberately preposterous statements to get his point across,"[7] creating absurd pictures of two-by-fours jutting out of people's eyes, camels getting their humps through the eye of Granny's needle, fastidious Pharisees straining bugs out of their soup with a camel-shaped object moving down their throats (see Matthew 7:4-5; 19:24; 23:24). (One wonders if the odd-looking camel was a favorite object of laughter by Jesus as far back as his toddlerhood in Egypt.)

Instead of using humor for entertainment's sake or to draw attention to himself, Jesus used it to *portray reality.* Full of surprise yet veracity, his unexpected and seemingly absurd paradoxical sayings[8] were true: Nicknaming the unstable, impetuous Simon "Rocky" (much like naming a black cat Snowball) became reality (see John 1:42). In this way, Jesus' humor was always profoundly full of deep meaning and always redemptive — pulling us back from our tendency toward sin in comic self-discovery: Every time I judge someone I'm straining out a gnat (their sin) and swallowing a camel (committing the sin of condemnation).

THE RESPONSE

Crowds flocked to hear Jesus. "People came to him" even after many rejected him (John 8:2, NRSV). They were "astounded at his teaching" and "listened to him with delight" (Matthew 7:28, NRSV; Mark 12:37). Josephus commented that Jesus' listeners "receive[d] the truth with pleasure"[9] He was not boring but dazzling.

People were drawn to him also because he "taught as one who had authority" (Matthew 7:29). By authority,

> the synoptic evangelists . . . are not merely referring
> to his tone of voice. . . . Instead of quoting learned
> authorities (or even debating the rights and
> wrongs of the opinions of some rabbinic school),
> he appeared to be founding a new school of his
> own. . . . He was not simply reshuffling the cards
> already dealt. He was more like a composer/
> conductor than a violin teacher.[10]

His messages were alarmingly different, yet they rang true. True authority has little to do with position or title (although it may accompany them).

> If the words that come from one's mouth are full
> of God's wisdom and insight, people notice and
> follow, regardless of the speaker's position, title,
> or diploma. This was what was so noticeable in
> Jesus, especially in contrast to the status-conscious
> Scribes and Pharisees (Matthew 7:28-29). The
> strongest and purest leaders do not need to rely
> upon position or title. Their passion, wisdom,
> and authentic love carry all the authority that is
> needed.[11]

Why? Because the wise love and loving wisdom of God create spiritual power in a person, and spiritual power is what we need (see Ephesians 3:16-20). Power and authority are based on one's way of serving others. When Jesus got up from washing the disciples' feet, he was more than ever before the most powerful person in the room.

Our Response: Being a Perpetual Student of Jesus

After this examination of Jesus as a teacher, a question presents itself: Am I willing to let Jesus be my teacher? Am I interested in spending my life being apprenticed to Jesus—learning from him how he might live his life if he were me—as a street cleaner, website designer, or botanist? Am I intensely curious about what Jesus was like, and do I want to carry knowledge of him within me?

Jesus as a brilliant teacher challenges us to *follow diligently*. He told us, "Learn from me" (Matthew 11:29, NRSV). God told Jesus' disciples, "Listen to him!" (Matthew 17:5, NRSV). We can become people who continually learn from Jesus, paying close attention to our lives and to our teaching (see 1 Timothy 4:16). In such a life we don't go to church to "get fed" (although that may happen at times), but we learn from Jesus every day in the midst of life, listening with our lives to God and absorbing God from the Word of God.

We apply our thinking powers to spiritual issues. We read the Bible for information but also for transformation. We don't try to finish a page or a chapter but read to let God speak to us, sitting in the quiet and letting the words sink into us. We respond to God by writing or saying, "Dear God" and seeing what flows from us next. We then pause and let God ask us questions. We put some of the scary things God says into practice so we can absorb what was really meant. We try living as if the Lord really is our shepherd—we try it on for size. Each day it fits a little better.

EXPERIMENTS IN CONNECTING WITH GOD
(Spiritual Practices to Consider)

To EXPERIENCE Jesus as our teacher for life

Meditation: Read Matthew 14:23-34 and picture it happening. Who does God invite you to become in this passage? How do you feel about what is happening? What do you want to say to Jesus?

Study: Investigate how Jesus used case studies, parables, everyday objects, and metaphors. Let yourself be fascinated by Jesus as a teacher.

Study: Read through a gospel in a day, noting everything about Jesus that surprises you, puzzles you, or fascinates you.

Welcoming strangers: When you meet someone new, open yourself to being taught something by that person (usually without his or her knowing it).

To BECOME Jesus' student for life

Fellowship: Ask someone with whom you're close to tell you what part of your life you need to pay more attention to (see 1 Timothy 4:16).

Intercessory prayer: Pray for a few people who might be in over their heads in a task. Ask God to empower them in the midst of this.

Meditation: How is Jesus asking you these questions today: "Do you believe I am able to transform you? To give you everything you need?" (see Psalm 23:1).

Reflection: Examine how you exercise authority in your life. How might you do so with less dominance and more wisdom, power, humility, and authentic love?

Reflection: What would help you "pay attention to your life"? Perhaps journaling, meeting with someone regularly to confess sins and pray together, taking Communion weekly or daily?

Service: Consider how you might need to show more latitude toward the people you serve.

Service: As an imparter of truth (either in informal conversations or teaching up front), how might you better use case studies, everyday objects, and metaphors?

Simplicity: As an imparter of truth, how might you need to say less but say it better?

Study: Read a classic book that is difficult for you. Don't worry if you don't understand *everything* in it. Pray about what you *do* understand.

Submission: Consider how asking questions requires more humility than telling people things.

Welcoming strangers: Examine your attitude toward people who ask a lot of questions, who challenge your thinking. What is your next step in being more welcoming of them?

QUESTIONS FOR DISCUSSION AND REFLECTION

1. Who have been your teachers about life? How did they do this — relationally or in the classroom? How well did they resemble Jesus?
2. Why is it scary to give latitude to a person you're teaching? What would help you do this?
3. Which of these teaching devices that Jesus used do you find most fascinating: case study, parables, everyday objects, or metaphors? Why?
4. What might you do in the next few days that would help you think more deeply?
5. Which of the experiments listed do you see yourself trying out this week?

❧

PART 4

JESUS, THE SELFLESS, HIDDEN SAVIOR

13   Hidden Servant

Imagine for a moment that you are Jesus' press agent. Think of how difficult it would be. How would you promote a popular celebrity who runs off during the perfect photo opportunity? How would you get his name into the newspaper or book him for speaking engagements when he doesn't schmooze with anyone? Picture this: Jesus has just provided food for thousands with no explainable source. So you're lining up reporters, political gatekeepers, and speaking circuit reps to interview him. There's talk of making him king or president. Where has he gone? Someone saw him scuttle his team off into a boat and head toward the mountains (see John 6:15). Surely not to pray. There's a time to pray and a time to act. This was a moment to seize the day.

Consider how handicapped you, as a press agent, would be because Jesus won't copiously display his powers. If you'd been hiding behind a rock during his temptations in the wilderness, no doubt you would have jumped out and pleaded with him to reconsider the Enemy's suggestion to jump off the peak of the temple. This is exactly the publicity break any up-and-coming preacher would want—a shortcut to greatness on the lecturing circuit. Think of how easy your job would be after that. Everyone would believe;

everyone would line up to invite Jesus to speak; everyone would fall down and worship him! Yet Jesus declined those who asked him for signs. Instead he referred to his upcoming death and resurrection (see Matthew 12:39-40). He made no effort to be a publicity magnet.

But possibly the worst situation for a press agent to endure would have been Jesus' behavior after the Resurrection: He did not appear to the people who had ridiculed him. Why didn't he swing by Pilate's house or stride through a session of the Sanhedrin? Then they would have believed. He missed his chance to say, "I told you so!"

Clearly Jesus was one who trafficked in hiddenness. Isaiah might have said about him what he said of God: "Truly you are a God who hides himself" (45:15). God's goodness is cloaked in mystery, inviting us to investigate and explore the depths of that goodness. For Jesus, power did not require or result in self-display. At times he even pictured the kingdom of God as small and hidden: a bit of yeast unrecognizable within a large amount of flour (but when worked through the lump of dough changes it completely; Matthew 13:33). Unlike power in the kingdoms of this world, God's kingdom power is not locked up in important positions or roles. Working in hiddenness, it shows up in people and places we consider insignificant (see 1 Corinthians 1:26-29).

AN ENCOUNTER WITH HIDDENNESS

Put yourself in the place of the two disciples walking to Emmaus (often thought to be Cleopas and his wife, Mary; Luke 24:13-35). You are grieving because you have watched the story of your people, Israel, play itself out in the life of Jesus. You're steeped in the history, the promises, and the prophecies, and you think it's time for God to deliver Israel from pagan oppression. You have high hopes for Israel, which is "a story in search of an ending." Jesus embodied these hopes, but his crucifixion was "the complete and final devastation of their hopes."[1] Just when all the signs were right, the liberator died. How could that be? The news of Jesus' missing body doesn't explain much. Where is that in the prophecies? As Cleopas or Mary, you are feeling sad, let down, and maybe even angry.

You meet a stranger on the road. He appears to know nothing about the high-drama trial and execution in Jerusalem, yet is oddly able to walk you through the Scriptures and show that Jesus' powerful but hidden kingdom is exactly what God promised. The "story was never about Israel beating up her enemies and becoming established as the high-and-mighty master of the world. It was always the story of how Israel's covenant God would save the world through the suffering and vindication of Israel."[2] When the stranger recasts the story this way, it shows how Moses and the prophets had really been talking about your friend Jesus as the true Israelite. The Cross was not *one more time* when paganism triumphed over your people Israel but "God's means of defeating evil once and for all."[3] The current events are exactly right after all. *Could it be?* you wonder.

This new perspective makes your heart burn within you—God really is on the move! The quickened rhythm of your steps on the road matches your rising heart rate as you walk. You've arrived home at Emmaus, and you want to keep talking about these things, but the stranger walks on without you. No! He must come with you and tell you more. So you stop him and invite him to eat with you. He agrees, but once in your home he doesn't behave like a proper guest. Instead he takes the role of host—picking up the bread, breaking it, and passing it to you. "In that glimpse of the way [your] friend always blessed and broke the bread, in that crack between heaven and earth, [you] see God. But it is only a glimpse. Then God is gone—but not gone."[4] Jesus is still with you, but hidden.

Spotting Jesus

The hidden Jesus still shows up today. We can be surprised and blessed "by the God who is expected but rarely appears where and when and how we imagine. It is God's way to come cloaked and also for his greatest promises to come cloaked."[5] But we have to be alert and watch carefully because Jesus "shows up" in small glimpses and then he's gone.

These glimpses occur most frequently for me with strangers at the Samaritan Center. Supposedly homeless persons (and maybe they are) show up only once (which is odd—we've had extremely regular daily clientele for thirteen years) and make a comment to me that I later realize was a blessing. One man looked at me intently and said, "I know God will use you in what it is you care about." Then he turned and walked out. This had happened with a few people by then, so I knew enough to run to the window to watch him walk away. I kept checking; he never came again. How did this stranger know I was discouraged about certain work projects? Why did he make that comment to me? We may have been talking about spiritual things (not an infrequent topic at the center), but he didn't know me. Such experiences train us to welcome strangers, not to "forget to entertain strangers, for by so doing some people have entertained angels without knowing it" (Hebrews 13:2).

In time, we learn to recognize those hands of Jesus breaking bread—or doing some other practical thing. If you're herding sheep, God might show up in a bush that burns too long. If you're a water-toting Palestinian woman, God might show up as a thirsty out-of-towner sitting at the well. If you're a swindler and manipulator, God might show up as a wrestler who makes sure your hip socket is never the same. The lives of Moses, the Samaritan woman, and Jacob demonstrate how God shows up in mundane moments and unexpected places. "God tends, by the logic of His creative effort, to make Himself sought and perceived by us . . . always on the alert to excite our first look and our first prayer."[6]

So we need to pay attention and respond. Moses had to ponder the continually burning bush and walk over to it. The Samaritan woman had to keep herself from smarting off to the Jew who didn't belong in her neighborhood but requested her help anyway. While

Jacob waited in the night at the Jabbok River, desperately stuck between a rock (Laban) and a hard-hearted brother (Esau), he had to wrestle his way into a blessing. God wants me to respond by participating in conversation with him. I confess I have looked for Jesus more diligently at the Samaritan Center than anywhere else. Why? Jesus tells us that when we feed the hungry, we're really doing it for him (see Matthew 25:40).

Sometimes I worry that this approach is too outlandish — not concrete and rational enough. So I'm relieved to remember that even the intellectual C. S. Lewis saw that "the world is crowded with [God]. He walks everywhere incognito. And the incognito is not always hard to penetrate. The real labour is to remember, to attend. In fact, to come awake. Still more, to remain awake."[7]

If you're awake, Jesus shows up in more conventional ways, especially in prayer and Bible reading and in the lives of people we know. I may thank a friend for something she said, but she doesn't remember saying it. When I teach, I'm no longer surprised that people thank me for saying certain phrases or ideas I didn't express. I use very detailed notes and remember what I insert so I know that I didn't say what blessed them. I now expect people to hear God in between the lines.

Like Cleopas and Mary, we need to keep our eyes open. Jesus will serve us in outlandish, practical, concrete ways. We are right to be astounded but to respect the hiddenness of his ways.

Jesus' Practice of Hiddenness

Jesus was not one to toot his own horn, sing his own praises, or work at making an impression. His refusal to show off demonstrated that love is not boastful, proud, or self-seeking (see 1 Corinthians 13:4-5). Here are some characteristic ways Jesus flew under the radar.

The secret helper. Running off after miraculously providing a crowd with food was typical. While he had strategic reasons for doing this (premature adulation would lead to a premature death), he made a habit of secrecy. After healing people, he frequently told them not to tell anyone (see Matthew 8:4; 9:30; Mark 3:12; 5:43; 7:36). While descending the mountain after appearing to the three disciples in his true glory, he told them not to speak about it until he rose from the dead (see Matthew 17:9). After turning the water into wine, he allowed the master of the banquet to give the credit for the superior quality of the wine to the bridegroom (see John 2:9-10). "Christ performed the necessary supernatural acts with a minimum of fanfare or extravagance. God receives *greater glory through quiet displays of divine power* than through superficial showmanship."[8]

The secret savior. Jesus' preference for divine hiddenness is revealed in his living in obscurity in Nazareth and in submission to his parents for so long. There's a saying that once you get a boy off the farm and into the city, you'll never get him back on the farm, but not so with Jesus. Even after his stimulating question-and-answer session astounded the teachers in the temple at the age of twelve, he willingly went back to his little hometown and submitted to his parents and to the obligations of an oldest son for eighteen more years (see Luke 2:46). During that time, the Savior of the world spent his days building chairs, beds, storage chests, oxen yokes, and even village homes. He could do everyday tasks and commercial endeavors "for the glory of God" (1 Corinthians 10:31).

THE WAY OF HIDDENNESS

In this age of self-promotion, common practice tells me to make myself look as good as I can on my résumé. I'm supposed to send out notices when my latest book is published. I'm supposed to drop names of famous people who attended the same meeting I did — "While I was talking to Billy, he mentioned that his crusade . . ." This is normal and expected — there are even classes on how to do this. Promoting ourselves is how we get ahead, which is the point for many of us.

If anyone could have been a show-off, it would have been Jesus.

Yet Jesus never used gimmicks to attract followers, to build a big attendance, or to make a name for himself. Even Jesus' family didn't understand, saying, "No one who wants to become a public figure acts in secret. Since you are doing these things, show yourself to the world" (John 7:4).

Jesus taught this secrecy and hiddenness with the funny picture of someone not letting his left hand know what his right hand is doing — as if that could be kept secret! Let's say your right hand helped an older person get out of a chair or massaged a sick person's back or wrote a check to a charity. Somehow you have to keep your left hand — just a few inches away — from knowing that the right hand just did this good deed. Try, really try, to keep your left hand from knowing. I'm sure that not even the people closest to Jesus knew half of the kindnesses he did.

Jesus was like the Father, the farmer who sows the field of the world refusing to dazzle us with irresistible powers. Three out of four soils find the powerful seed of the kingdom easy to resist. God doesn't overpower us but lets us choose. Such is the nature of love. It doesn't force, it doesn't coerce, it doesn't push.

> [God] is unwilling to impose himself on anyone
> if and as long as that can be avoided. He will not
> force himself upon you, He will not jump down
> your throat. . . . In *The Screwtape Letters*,
> C. S. Lewis has the senior devil, Screwtape, say to
> his protégé, Wormwood, . . . "the creatures are to
> be one with Him, but yet themselves."[9]

Leaving Our Freedom Intact

God's hiddenness meets the human need for space to choose. I often think of Jesus as behaving like a prince in a fairy tale who masquerades as a poor, itinerant farm worker or shepherd boy, roaming from place to place hoping to find a woman who will love him for his own self—without the trappings of a palace, royal clothing, servants, and presents. If the girl he chooses to love knows the shepherd boy is really a prince, she might be overwhelmed by his power and status and so agree to marry him without loving him at all. Or she might feel forced to marry him because of his status. But she doesn't know all these wonderful things about him—she just knows him!—so she can decide for herself if she loves him. That's what Jesus wants: for you to choose him, to love God *for God's own self* without being overwhelmed or forced to do so. Indeed, Jesus used this theme of the masquerading royalty in his account of a king who says that if you helped the "least of these," you were really doing it for him (Matthew 25:40,35-36, KJV).

God remains hidden enough for us to make our own decisions without undue influence. That means we can *freely choose God.* "What would happen to our freedom if God, our perfect lover, were to appear before us with such objective clarity that our doubts disappeared? . . . It would be love like a reflex. . . .True love is born of freedom . . . and also of difficult choices."[10] I had strange feelings of God puncturing this hiddenness and making that Divine Wonderfulness much too obvious when I visited Alaska. Vistas of its mountains, glaciers, and seas made me exclaim, "At this point the angels must have said during creation, 'This is too much! Stop now—or humans will never need faith!'" Such beauty provides almost too much evidence of God's goodness and creative power. No wonder it's tucked away in a sparsely populated area. "God is so great that in order for us to avoid him, he has to hide from us."[11]

God Wants Us to Choose

God's hiddenness invites us to decide if we want God for God's own self—or if we simply want a secure future in eternity and abundant life now. God is more than a ticket to heaven or a key to fulfillment today. Like the masquerading prince, "God *wants to be wanted* and tries not to be manifestly present where he is not wanted." And like the prince who leaves clues to his identity — something he knows or does that only the prince could know or do — "God lets himself be known, for example, in the story and person of Jesus. He is available to those who really *want* him. 'When you search for me, you will find me; if you seek me with all your heart' (Jeremiah 29:13)."[12]

God waits for us to choose. Instead of pushing his way in, Jesus waits to be invited. He did not assume Cleopas and Mary wished him to come home with them. When they neared their village, he "acted as if he were going on but they pressed him" (Luke 24:28-29, MSG). Part of the way we seek God with all our heart is to arrange our life in such a way that we are connecting with God as many minutes of the day as possible. We learn to watch for God's hiddenness in the world and relish practicing hiddenness and secrecy as we abide in Christ.

EXPERIMENTS IN CONNECTING WITH GOD
(Spiritual Practices to Consider)

To RECEIVE from God the joy of being hidden in Christ

Celebration: Thank God for seemingly hidden people who have helped you in the past: people who have prayed for you; authors who have written books that have helped you; people at church who have seen you and blessed you as you've walked by.

Meditation: Read Colossians 3:1-4 slowly and then read verses 3-4 (in italics) slowly several times. See what words stand out:

> Since, then, you have been raised with Christ, set
> your hearts on things above, where Christ is seated
> at the right hand of God. Set your minds on things
> above, not on earthly things. *For you died, and your*

life is now hidden with Christ in God. When Christ,
who is your life, appears, then you also will appear
with him in glory.

Ponder what is good about being "hidden with Christ in God."

Meditation: Read Luke 24:13-35 and picture it happening. See yourself as one of the two disciples walking and being served. How do feel about what is happening? What do you want to say to Jesus?

Practicing the presence of God: Pay attention to the people around you. How is God showing up in them — especially the strangers?

Prayer: Talk with God about something good that you've done that no one else knows about. Sense God's pleasure in you and God's power working in you.

Reflection: How has God served you in hidden ways today? What "minor miracles" have occurred? What frustrating circumstances have you turned over to God and then seen resolved?

Secrecy: Pray for someone you feel in competition with — for his or her well-being and success.

Study and meditation: Find the six references in Psalms to finding shelter under God's wings (usually in the "shadow" of his wings). Consider the hiddenness involved in this image. Of these references, which phrases are most inviting to you? Why?

Welcoming strangers: Try being warm and inviting to the most pitiful people you can find. Look into their eyes, remembering the masquerading king saying, "I was a stranger and you welcomed me."

Worship: Take a walk and sing or hum the hymn (especially verse 2) "How Great Thou Art." Consider how God uses nature to reveal himself and yet to conceal himself.

To BECOME content in hiddenness

Confession: Speak with someone (or journal this) you trust about the times you want to show off, drop names, or impress people. What lurks within you that causes this?

Prayer and secrecy: Pray for someone for several days, but do not tell this person about it. Let it be a secret between you and God.

Recollection: Near the end of the day, consider where God may have been working in your life in hidden ways that day.

Secrecy: Ask God to show you how you could help someone secretly—perhaps giving the person money (through your church) or saying something good about someone to advance his or her cause.

Secrecy: Avoid telling someone about the good thing you did.

Service and secrecy: Once a day do some small thing that no one will probably see: Make a roommate's bed; pick up trash on the sidewalk.

Silence: Refrain from saying anything about yourself all day long (or maybe for only an hour).

Silence: Go to a meeting where opinions will be asked for. Commit yourself not to speak unless asked a question. Instead pray fervently for each person there.

QUESTIONS FOR DISCUSSION AND REFLECTION

1. How would you have felt if you had been Cleopas or Mary in these moments?
   - When you first started walking and encountered a stranger who didn't know about the Crucifixion
   - When the stranger began explaining the Scriptures and Jesus' life like a jigsaw puzzle fitting together
   - When the stranger disappeared—you're sitting there with the bread still in your hand

2. Whom do you know who doesn't show off but has so many reasons they could?
3. Where might you be Jesus (the stranger) in other people's lives?
4. What does this chapter lead you to want to pray?
5. Which of the experiments listed do you see yourself trying out this week?

14   Dying to Self

Why is it that Jesus asks me to do the reverse of what smart, clever, successful people have taught me? For instance . . .

Career. A professional writers' organization taught me to advance my career by networking and "getting my name out there," but Jesus didn't let me feel right about this. The more I put myself forward, the cheaper I felt. The more I tried to be somebody, the less I could hear God. The more I networked, the more guilty I felt for using people instead of loving them.

Marriage. Christian authors told me how to get my husband to meet my needs, but Jesus revealed to me that I was using my husband to get what I wanted. Instead God challenged me to see my husband's heart and cherish it and to love him by doing little things for him in the next ten minutes.

Friendship. I was told that in order to have friends, I needed to be a good friend, but Jesus challenged me to love the person in front of me, expecting no token of friendship in return.

Self. Christian books and conferences urged me to love myself and offered me various keys to fulfillment, but the Holy Spirit invited me to stop thinking about self and taste daily the self-giving love of God.

God. The world and the church hinted if not outright said, "You get points for trying," but Jesus asked me simply to abide in him and he would take care of the fruit. Jesus said it wasn't about performance. "Die to yourself," I could hear him say. "That's what *I* did. Will you?"

THE RADICAL SELFLESSNESS OF JESUS

Jesus did not focus his life on getting his needs met. He could have turned stones into bread during the temptations, but he didn't. When the woman at the well hesitated to share a cup with him, he could have created an instant well to satisfy his thirst, but he didn't. When the officers came to arrest him in Gethsemane, he could have called ten thousand angels to scare them, but he didn't (Matthew 4:2-4; John 4:9; 18:2-12).

Instead of putting himself forward, Jesus followed a public relations policy based on attraction rather than promotion. He did not lure, convince, or manipulate people, thus crossing their spiritual boundaries, but he let them choose or not choose to follow him. Jesus didn't look for glory or perform for human credit but ordered the crowds he had cured "not to make him known" (see Matthew 12:16,19-20, NRSV).

Emptying of self was Jesus' way: "Christ Jesus: Who, being in very nature God, did not consider equality with God something to be grasped, but *made himself nothing*, taking the very nature of a servant, being made in human likeness. And being found in appearance as a man, he humbled himself and became obedient to death — even death on a cross!" (Philippians 2:5-8, italics added).

Jesus lampooned self-absorption in his ridiculous parable of the guy who was forgiven millions but couldn't forgive pennies. This guy lived with his head in a bucket, in a world of only himself. He saw himself as a victim, first of the master who wanted to be paid back and then of the slave who could not pay him back. His attitude shows how self-absorption skews our view of how people treat us. Eager to insert clarity into the story, Jesus brought in the other servants, who reported to the master the inconsistent servant's behavior. I'm sure our main character was shocked that others thought he had done wrong (see Matthew 18:23-34).

Self-Absorption: Today's Disease

When living in a state of self-absorption, we want what we want when we want it. We may not perceive this in ourselves, yet it reveals itself when we don't get our way. If we don't like a decision, it's okay to put people down or manipulate them to get them to agree with us. If we're not recognized sufficiently, it's okay to exaggerate. If we're overlooked by a clerk, it's okay to become sarcastic.

When our wants are ultimate, we congratulate ourselves as being persuasive or skilled as an arm-twister. We may control loved ones or feel cheated about not being able to afford certain items. Competition is often involved (though not admitted), which is often about the "pleasure of being above the rest."[1]

Evelyn Underhill said it well: "We mostly spend [our] lives conjugating three verbs: to *want*, to *have*, and to *do*. Craving, clutching and fussing . . . , we are kept in perpetual unrest."[2] In so doing, we worship a false trinity: power, possessions, human relationships.[3] We're willing to sacrifice almost anything to get them:

- *Power:* spending time and money on appearance and clothes as sources of acceptance; spending hours planning what to say to convince a friend, our boss, or the pastor to see things our way
- *Possessions:* incurring credit card debt and making up for it with overwork
- *Certain human relationships:* feeling incapable of saying no to certain people; acting in certain ways around influential people to impress them

The spiritualized wording of worshipping this false trinity is to act in these ways but call it "trusting God for things." But our trust is that God will *give us what we want!* We may excuse ourselves for this because we want only good things: to help my church or serve my family. In reality, we're trusting ourselves: "I am *my own shepherd* and I hunt down what I need. I create *my own green pastures and still waters* — even if I have to steal someone else's grass, water, or peace to get them."

CHRISTIANITY'S FORGOTTEN CALL

In contemporary Christianity, "death to self" is not a commonly discussed topic. Theologian Simon Chan observed, "In much of contemporary American culture, aggressive self-regard is no longer viewed with alarm."[4] Aggressive self-regard is now *the norm*.

In contrast, death to self is about being crucified with Christ daily (see Galatians 2:20). (It is not to be confused with death *of* self, because God doesn't want to blot us out or make us disappear. God treasures each of us and respects us.) Death to self is releasing the desire to have things my way and being open to how God leads me today. It makes way for the eternal kind of life that we were born for. If we die to self-absorption, the best in us will emerge: "Christ in you, the hope of glory" (Colossians 1:27). Not focusing on self gives us time and strength to pay attention to what's really important.

Death to self leads to real life. Consider the concept of death leading to life in these passages: Only if a grain of wheat *dies* in the earth will it rise up and *bear much fruit*; only if we *lose our life* will we experience an *eternal kind of life*; only as we *carry around in our bodies the death of Jesus* will the *life of Jesus be revealed* in our bodies; only as my *life becomes hidden with Christ in God* will I be *revealed with Christ in glory*; only as I become *like Jesus in his death* will I participate in a *resurrected sort of life* here and now today (see John 12:24-25; 2 Corinthians 4:10; Colossians 3:3-4; Philippians 3:10-11;

see also Romans 6:3-8; 2 Corinthians 5:15; Galatians 2:20). Such death to self and subsequent glorious life in Christ does happen at physical death but it also happens now. We die to ourselves daily and live to Christ daily, even minute by minute.

What Does Death to Self Look Like?

As we participate in the death-to-self sessions of soul school, the self-sins fade: self-righteousness, self-pity, self-sufficiency[5] (not referring to sensible self-care but *devotion* to self). Habits of self-pity become transformed into empathy. We move from a victim identity to compassionately identifying with others.

No longer wanting to have our way: It becomes easier to treat others as we wish to be treated and refuse to do whatever it takes to get our needs met. Instead we ask God to meet our needs. As we no longer try to make things happen, we let go of the desire to control others and the need to be right.

No longer concerned about what others think of us: We are released from the bondage of wanting people to like us. It's okay for you not to have a good opinion of me. In fact, I accept that there are legitimate reasons for people not to have a good opinion of me. That makes it easier for me to confess my sins and come clean with my faults. Transparency, authenticity, and vulnerability become second nature.

No longer trying to get people to look up to us: Jesus "made himself of no reputation" and did not miss it (Philippians 2:7, KJV). We no longer worry about getting honor and credit, saying, "I was the one who told her that, you know." Death to self teaches us to be okay when I see others praised but I am overlooked. It's okay to be last.

No longer thinking I know best: As we join Jesus in death to self, we stop "should-ing" on people and telling them what to do: You should read this book; you should go to this conference. We respect people more and listen to their ideas.

No longer defending self: When attacked, we practice silence instead of explaining, "I just did that because . . ." or "I don't want you to think . . ." We no longer try to manage others' opinions of us. This lack of defensiveness also helps us understand that we are not necessarily being mistreated. These people aren't mad at me; they're just having a bad day. We find we're less filled with anger and contempt.

No longer looking to see if I get the response I'd hoped for: When making a request, I can simply state my needs and see what happens. If the person is unable to meet them, I trust that God will meet my needs in another way. This keeps us from evaluating whether others reciprocate when we reach out in friendship. It keeps us from feeling hurt because people do not listen deeply after we give them a listening ear. We give without worrying about what we receive in return.

No longer obsessed with self: Self-preoccupation is a result of pride, a vice that "every one in the world loathes when he sees it in someone else"[6] yet rarely spots in oneself. This pride is replaced with humility, which practically speaking, means that we never push, we never pretend, and we never presume.[7] To never push is to respect others' personhood. To never pretend is to be just who we are, no more or no less; we don't pretend to know more, saying, "I read that book." To never presume is to stop thinking I deserve more than I do; it's to pray for the people around me instead of presuming to be the Holy Spirit in their lives by giving them unsought advice.

Does "death to self" sound too hard? It's easier than living for self. When we straddle the fence trying to live for both God and self, we constantly feel guilty and inadequate. Every temptation creates a war in our head: Will we give in or not? Life in Christ becomes a dreary, foot-dragging trudge through the mud. But if instead of trying to be good, we stay connected with God through spiritual practices, we will find that the yoke is easy and the burden is light. As we die to self, we have the companionship of God and live an eternal life now.

Participating in Jesus' Death and Jesus' Life

Jesus' death on the cross is the ultimate symbol of death to self. The Cross was not a moment of defeat but a moment when Jesus showed great love and submission to the will of the Father "for the joy set before him" (Hebrews 12:2). Several of the sculpted stations of the cross at a local retreat center insightfully portray Jesus *embracing* the cross with a look of loving purposeful intentionality. He was not a victim. Embracing this cross was his act of self-giving love for a world full of self-importance and in need of selflessness.

To be crucified *with* Christ, then, means that we also embrace this death. As Oswald Chambers put it, we become broken bread and poured-out wine in the hands of Jesus Christ.[8] While this might require our physical death, it will more likely require that we die daily with Christ (see 1 Corinthians 15:31). It must have shocked the disciples to watch Jesus die to self each day, often in service to them.

WATCHING JESUS

In the hours before the trial and the Crucifixion, Jesus enacted death to self in a most appalling way (see John 13:1-17). Washing feet was the filthy work of a slave because sandal-shod feet, as the primary means of transportation in biblical times, got dirty and injured in this dusty land. Consider that if the tires of your car regularly rolled across your carpet or kitchen floor, you'd keep them very clean.

Picture the disciples at the Last Supper arguing again about who would be considered the greatest, an apparent favorite topic (see Luke 22:24-38). As they discuss their rights and privileges and what they deserve, Jesus thinks tenderly that "having loved his own who were in the world, he now show[s] them the *full extent of his love*" (John 13:1, italics added). His mind focuses on that sublime mutual submission of his obeying the Father and the Father putting *all* things in his hands (see verse 3).

The next moment is one of the most dramatic in Scripture. Jesus gets up, takes off his outer clothing (imagine the gasps), and wraps a towel around his waist—apparently without explanation. The rest of them are fully clothed but their master is not, even with women nearby (no doubt to serve). This meager dress foreshadows his complete nakedness on the cross within a matter of hours.

The disciples are undoubtedly horrified for their teacher to behave like a slave. Washing feet is to them as emptying a slop bucket or chamber pot would be to us. The scene is backward: A rabbi's disciples were supposed to render personal service for their teacher, but instead their teacher is serving them. Apparently no slave is there to do this work, and not one of them has volunteered because the task is too lowly.

Put yourself in this passage as a disciple. How do you feel as you watch Jesus move around the group? How do you feel as he comes toward you? What are you thinking?

As Jesus comes to wash your feet, hear the basin being moved and feel the water pouring over your feet as they're rubbed tenderly. You're used to looking up at Jesus standing in front of people or on a hilltop. How does it feel to look down on Jesus in this vulnerable position—one in which many slaves were no doubt kicked? Does it remind you of a man proposing marriage, of Jesus wooing us into union with God? One time as I meditated on this I began sobbing. Another time I saw myself falling into Jesus' arms as he washed my feet.

For a moment, imagine Jesus washing Judas's feet. What might Jesus be praying for Judas? What does Jesus' face look like—knowing his character as you do?

Now be an onlooker as Jesus moves to Peter. He refuses to let Jesus wash his feet. When Jesus says that he'll understand later, Peter isn't satisfied. Have you noticed how often Peter tells Jesus what to do: Don't wash my feet; wash all of me? Earlier Peter brashly insisted that Jesus would never be killed and rise again—even though Jesus said so! It seems that nobody, not even Peter, "gets" Jesus. We are blessed if there is even one person on the planet who truly understands us. If Jesus has that someone who understands him, it isn't one of these guys. But Jesus is practiced at having the companionship of the Father and escapes for times of solitude (with God) even here on earth.

Consider the manner in which Jesus washes their feet, moving around the group. Using the adjectives of 1 Corinthians 13:4-8, we can guess he moves with *patience*. Twelve people are not too many. Jesus is not hurried. With *kindness*, he pays attention to the tough places in their feet. *Without envy* or *pride*, he doesn't congratulate himself on his humility. He isn't trying to shame them or show them up. He *is not rude*, making jokes about their feet or how dirty they are. Each foot is a dear part of someone he loves. Even with Peter's antics, he is *not easily irritated*. He doesn't think, *This guy is impossible!* He enacts the living truth of love and humility right before them.

When Jesus finishes and puts his clothes back on, he breaks the silence by telling them he has set a pattern for them: Love is willing to do whatever is needed, no matter how menial (see John 13:15). "The truly Christlike leader is known by the ease and spontaneity with which he or she does the little, annoying, messy things . . . the things which in our world we always secretly hope someone else will do so we won't have to waste our time, to demean ourselves."[9]

How can Jesus submit to his disciples this way? Because he knows who he is: He comes from God and returns to God (see verse 3). He lives with the companionship of the Father even on earth, as you and I also are meant to live now. Jesus' action illustrates that selfless service doesn't just happen. It doesn't come from nowhere. It flows from the resource of the companionship of God's self-giving love.

But I'll Never Be Jesus

This passage may sadden us to think that our self-absorbed behavior is so far from Jesus' selfless behavior. We might beat ourselves up, thinking, *I'll never be like this!* or comfort ourselves by saying, "Nobody's perfect." Rather than focusing on our failures, it's wiser to connect with God.

First, we can fall down on our faces and *worship* Jesus that he is so far beyond us — Jesus really is God! We can pray that we will "grasp [a little of] how wide and long and high and deep is the love of Christ" (Ephesians 3:18). Lewis counseled that this results in humility: "If you really get into any kind of touch with [God] you will, in fact, be humble — delightedly humble, feeling the infinite relief of having for once got rid of all the silly nonsense about your own dignity which has made you restless and unhappy all your life."[10]

Another response is to *confess* our inadequacy and ask God, *Is there a "next step" for me?* Admittedly, it will be an almost-nothing step compared to Christ's magnificent behavior, but we ask, *What is my next step to "Christ in me — the hope of glory"? What are you leading me to do to die to self?* Here are some next steps that have helped me.

SPIRITUAL DISCIPLINES TO DIE TO SELF

Disciplines of abstinence teach us to die to self and liberate us to "do it all for the glory of God" (1 Corinthians 10:31). For example, *secrecy* — abstaining from letting our good deeds be known — keeps us from pride. Combined with *selfless service,* it frees us from living by the opinions of others and doing things to be approved by certain people. *Solitude* drains us of pride because it keeps us from being productive for a short while. Disciplines of situational *silence* (not having the last word, not giving one's opinion unless asked) keep me from focusing on self.

Fasting is a key discipline in dying to self. Abstaining from all food or from desserts or chocolate (or from watching television or from media) helps us practice being sweet instead of grouchy when we don't get what we want. Can I still be strong and cheerful by the strengthening of the Holy Spirit? Can I trust God instead of feeling deprived (and therefore mistreated)?

Frugality also helps us die to desires to indulge ourselves. If you want to buy something, wait a year. Make do with what you have. Relish old, well-worn items instead of buying something new. Learn to be at peace without getting more.

As with all disciplines, start small. Don't be heroic. Enjoy the results of practicing disciplines of abstinence: You don't hurry so much; you have more inner quiet and more time to love people; you become more content because you're okay with not having what you were sure you wanted.

EXPERIMENTS IN CONNECTING WITH GOD
(Spiritual Practices to Consider)

To ABSORB death to self and a resurrected sort of life from God

Associating with the lowly: Interact with (or at least observe) a poor person in some way, asking yourself, *Why didn't Jesus resent being poor?*

Meditation: Read John 13:1-17 and picture it happening. Write down the feelings you would have had if you had been one of the disciples, especially Judas. Jot down anything else about Jesus that comes to you.

Meditation: Insert your name in the blanks and hear Jesus say to you, "___, I want you to truly know me. I want to give you spiritual power — resurrection sort of power. This will mean you have to let go of quite a bit, especially those things you regard as success. But you won't be sorry because you'll bask in the surpassing richness of knowing me as your all in all. You'll need to lay aside certain things that look good (and you'll see how silly it was to hold on to them) so that you can gain more of me and make me your own. It will gradually become clear to you and others that you are mine — not because you do good things but because you radiate a self-forgetful, unassuming goodness that can come only from me.

"Now, _____, you aren't there yet, but press in; don't give up because I've got a hold of you and I am doing this *in you*. You're going to have to forget, to let go of, and to lay aside the glories (and faults) of yesterday, last year, and ten years ago and then turn your attention and energy toward me and the with-God life I'm drawing you into. Trust me more than ever before" (see Philippians 3:7-14, beginning with verse 10).

Reflection: Journal about how God dies to self in not imposing things on you, in giving you latitude to make mistakes.

To BECOME one who lives death to self and a resurrected sort of life

Confession: Write down situations in which you feel like a victim: when people don't return your phone calls; when people aren't grateful for what you've done; when people who owe you money don't pay you back.

Fasting: As you abstain from food (or media), journal about how it feels to not get what you want. Use these breath prayers: "strong and cheerful" or "trusting God today."

Fasting: Each time you feel hungry, pray for someone in need — perhaps in a war-torn area. (Choose this group or situation the night before.)

Frugality (simplicity): Choose not to buy something you planned to buy. How does it feel to wait and do without?

Frugality: Set a specific number of days you will not shop. In the time normally spent shopping, do something you usually don't have time to do.

Practicing the presence of God: Experiment with using this breath prayer: "More of Jesus" (inhale), "less of me" (exhale). What would be some ideal moments to practice this?

Secrecy: Go out of your way to keep a good deed from being known.

Simplicity: Cut down on your work hours (if applicable). Are you
    okay with achieving less?

Solitude: Set aside time to be alone. Start with ten minutes, a morn-
    ing, a whole day, a few days, a week. Notice how it quiets you
    and you learn to love the companionship of God.

Silence: Ask God to help you with one of these situational disciplines
    of silence: not having the last word, not giving your opinion
    unless asked. Keep a journal on how it goes, but don't worry
    about doing it perfectly. Most of all, what do you learn about
    what goes on inside you?

Submission: Give in to someone you rarely give in to. Let the person
    have his or her way.

Submission: Do something that someone has told you would be a
    good idea. Perhaps you didn't think so at the time, but give it
    a try.

Welcoming strangers: Journal about how you practice hospitality. Do
    you hope to make people feel at home and safe with you, or do
    you attempt to offer a perfect picture of your home or self in
    order to make a good impression?

QUESTIONS FOR DISCUSSION AND REFLECTION

1. What does this chapter lead you to want to pray?
2. In what situations is it considered normal to push your own
    agenda (perhaps for the sake of family members or even
    religion)?
3. If the role of persuasion is not to convince people against their
    will (arm twisting), when is it appropriate?
4. When are you most likely to feel overlooked or ignored? When
    would it be appropriate to die to self?
5. Which of the experiments listed do you see yourself trying out
    this week?

15   Slow to Speak

As my friend rehearsed for me what she planned to say to her husband, I could see myself in her approach. She built her case, presented her view, and left no clever phrase unsaid. She raised her voice to emphasize her point, lowered her voice to appear agreeable, and paused dramatically when nothing else worked. She asked me if I thought she would be convincing. I offered, "How about if you 'say it short,' grin, and be quiet? Then walk away and let him think about it."

Like my friend, I have for years presented ideas with a song, a dance, and snazzy flair. But as I became a mother of teenagers (the experience-based classroom that taught me, "say it short"), I saw that my approach revealed my lack of trust that God would work unless I pushed. To be people who are "quick to listen" and "slow to speak" (James 1:19), we need to let the Lord be our shepherd enough to develop a less-is-more, understated way of speaking.

While communication is important, talking has its limits. With elaborate facial expressions and hand gestures, we make sure coworkers or children know we *mean what we say*. When feeling insecure, overlooked, or slighted, we use words to win people over or to prove our sincerity. Jesus' instruction sounds so radical to a world that routinely speaks in exclamation points: "Simply let your 'Yes' be 'Yes,' and your 'No,' 'No'" (Matthew 5:37). Really?

Jesus taught this radical notion in a culture in which "evasive swearing" was common. Good Jews could swear by anything — heaven, earth, Jerusalem, or even their own head — but the oath was not binding if they didn't use the name of God (see Matthew 5:33-36).[1] As a result, they could lace their statements with strong wording to influence others but have no intention of following through. They were still being technically honest even though they spoke with a deceitful heart.

But isn't it wimpy not to put our ideas forward in a convincing way? Consider that speaking concisely has its own power. In writing about Quaker leader George Fox, William Penn said, "The *fewness* and *fullness* of his words have often struck even strangers with admiration."[2] Fewness. Fullness. Not only did George Fox speak little, but when he did speak, his carefully chosen words welled up from the simplicity of his heart, creating a clear and compelling effect.

SIMPLY PUT

Jesus was not given to gushy speeches or explaining himself but to brevity of words. Consider the royal official who must have been used to wowing others as he begged Jesus to *come with him* — asking twice — to heal his son (see John 4:47,49). In response to these entreaties, Jesus didn't make excuses, nor did he go with him, but he uttered these simple words: "You may go. Your son will live" (verse 50). These brief words convinced the official: He "believed the word that Jesus spoke to him and started on his way" (verse 50, NRSV).

Jesus' brief words and simple actions impressed others as having authority partly because he, unlike others, wasn't trying to impress anyone. When the demon-possessed man called out to him as he taught in the Capernaum synagogue, he said only, "Be quiet! Come out of him!" (Mark 1:25), but witnesses were impressed with his authority (see Mark 1:22,27). In his healings and exorcisms he avoided the routine razzle-dazzle. While "ordinary Jewish and pagan exorcists used elaborate incantations, and spells, and magical rites, Jesus with clear, simple, brief [words of] authority exorcised the demon from the man. No one had ever seen anything like this before."[3] Perhaps emphasizing this, Mark went on to describe how simply Jesus healed Peter's mother-in-law. Instead of using the complicated system laid down in the Talmud of healing a burning fever with use of paraphernalia, gestures, and successive repeating of certain phrases from the law,[4] Jesus simply "helped her up" (Mark 1:31).

The Simplicity of Silence

Jesus shows us how even in fiery situations, staying silent is often the best choice. It gives us time to hear God and creates space in which our conversation partner might also hear God. Perhaps that was what Jesus was up to in one of his most famous moments of silence — an episode we've considered before but will now view from another angle.

Put yourself in the crowded temple when people whom every Jew looks up to — Pharisees and teachers of the law — drag forth a woman "caught in adultery" (John 8:1-11). Perhaps her hair is disheveled and she is hiding within a blanket thrown over her. Tension fills the air as they make her stand before them. Where is she looking? Probably at the ground. They are using her as a tool to trap Jesus — will he grant mercy (which seemed to violate the law) or do justice (then he would not be a "friend of sinners")?

But Jesus knew that not every demand requires an answer, especially an answer framed according to the demand. When people ask us to take sides, that doesn't mean we have to. Instead of answering, Jesus squats in the sand and writes in it with his finger. To our frustration, what he writes is not recorded. Some have suggested that he didn't write words but just doodled. Others have suggested that because the word for "write" is *katagrapho* (meaning "write against" or "accuse"), Jesus wrote each of their sins before them in the sand.[5] Or perhaps the words aren't recorded because quite mystically each person looks at what Jesus writes and sees different words — exact words that convict them to release their rocks.

Jesus' silence works. It gives them time to think and ponder like a child being given a time-out in the corner. It forces them to repeat their demands, to which Jesus tells them to go ahead and stone her if their consciences will let them. But instead of sermonizing, he squats and writes again. His silence allows their cruel words to ring in the air right there in God's temple. It is as if he is saying, "Listen to your murderous words. How do you judge yourselves?" "His [in]action created a tomb-like silence in which men fear to move or breathe. He had challenged them to kill her, but He knew they would flee from the ghosts of their own consciences."[6] Inactivity, silence, and brevity of speech give people space to hear themselves.

Jesus doesn't seem to think, *Since I'm an important prophet, I'd better comment about this.* Or, *Here's a chance to spar with my enemies!* because this is, after all, a high-drama media event in a strategic location. Jesus' opponents may feel frustrated at this point. How do you antagonize someone whose buttons will not be pushed?

When Jesus does speak, he doesn't take sides or give an opinion but speaks to the needs of the persons involved. He meets the Pharisees' and teachers' needs by forcing them to listen to themselves as he occupies himself in silence. He meets the woman's needs by offering her forgiveness and inviting her to a new way of life. Loving people and speaking to their needs is usually better than taking sides. Because Jesus came from outside the box, he thought outside the box.

THE HEART EXAM

Just as the silence of Jesus seems to have led Jesus' opponents to examine their hearts, Jesus hinted at the need for a heart exam in the midst of chatter: "Anything beyond this [the simple yes and no]

comes from the evil one" (Matthew 5:37). What thoughts are behind
our excessive words? As I began a slow-to-speak project in soul
school, I was surprised by what surfaced in my journal:

> As I abstain from chatter and "overtalk," I see that
> I have used words to get my way, to get attention,
> or to get the credit I'm afraid others won't give me.
> I do it because I am concerned about what others
> think and I want to make a good impression. This
> self-preoccupation is subtle, but it's there. I have
> to be very quiet to hear it rising up within me.
> Sometimes I can't hear it at all, but I know it's there
> because of how I feel after I over-talk—awkward,
> dissatisfied, knowing I entered a state in which God
> was not the biggest thing in my life.

Words are the primary vehicles we use to shape our image and
get our way. We may not pressure someone with the point of a gun,
but we do it with the point of our words. Without realizing it, we use
words and facial expressions to dominate, especially by interrupting,
exaggerating, or choosing dramatic (or spiritual-sounding) words.
If others don't believe us or seem convinced they should do what we
want, we speak more forcefully. Often we do this because we think
we're right or to defend ourselves. In the meantime, our speech is
drained of love and respect for others. Our heart has stopped trusting God to work in the situation, so we help God out with our ready
supply of persuasive words.

Awhile ago, I was serving alongside some dear people who asked
if I'd be attending a concert they were giving. I smiled and said no.
Even though I'd never attended their concerts before, they seemed
to wait for me to offer a reason for not coming. I felt extreme pressure within myself to explain that I'd been traveling a lot and that I
was reserving that day for a Sabbath. But I also knew that if I tried

to explain myself, I would probably launch into one of my mini-lectures on practicing a Sabbath. So instead I grinned again and asked them about their plans for the event. By not explaining myself, I knew I was risking their thinking that I was a flake or that I didn't care about them. As I listened attentively to their plans, I prayed that my interest would communicate the love I was eager to give these fine people.

Heart Issues

Simplicity of speech usually flows from a heart that mirrors the heart of Jesus: compassion and truth, love and goodness. Our words reveal what is already stored in our heart (see Matthew 12:34-35). If I am putting confidence in myself instead of God, it will show itself in the force and volume of my words. But as I mirror the heart of Christ, my heart will direct my mouth to state an idea briefly and peacefully and then allow others full freedom to respond.

Some might object that talkativeness is not a heart issue but a personality trait. Aren't some people just chatty? If so, this trait needs to be used as a gift from God to bless others. Good stewardship of this gift means pausing before saying what pops into our head and thinking about how it will affect others. This is especially true with a close friend or spouse because we tend to be more careless and long-winded with them.

To attempt simplicity of speech isn't easy because our mouth feels as if it can't help itself and our tongue seems to have a life of its own. If you don't think so, try to stop interrupting or raising your voice when you feel as if no one is hearing you or inserting little jokes and plays on words even if it causes others to shut down. This struggle with words is often magnified for those who talk for a living (teachers, pastors, speakers, sales reps). If people listen attentively to us when we're presenting on a platform, shouldn't they also be spellbound in private conversation?

Loving Others and Trusting God

In my own heart-exam odyssey, I admit that at first I simply tried to talk less. But as usual, focusing on what we shouldn't do doesn't help. What works better is to love the person standing in front of us, asking ourselves, *How can I draw others into conversation? How is the Spirit nudging me to love the people around me and hear their deeper selves in this moment?* (If people tell you that you don't talk enough, these two questions might help you.) If we connect with God this way, the perfecting is more likely to flow from us.

Such prayers help our speech become a way of showing love, of which respect is a core rhythm. As we practice eager listening and slow speaking, we become fully present to others without thinking of what we want to say next. Steady practice of simple speech retrains us to set those thoughts aside, fix our gaze on the other person, and consider deeply what that person is saying. We see the face of Christ superimposed on that individual's face (see Matthew 25:37-40) and wonder with joy at the person God has put in our life at that moment.

Such practice turns us into people who ask questions more than offer opinions. Our yes or no can be depended on because we're becoming people whose talk demonstrates the Spirit's power instead of clever eloquence (see 1 Corinthians 2:2-5).

This practice also trains us to have confidence that God works without our over-the-top efforts. I don't have to toot my own horn because I can trust God with my reputation. I can state my boundaries briefly without scolding others because I trust that God will not let me be walked on or ignored. I can trust the Lord as my shepherd today and move along believing that God will provide everything I need.

Retraining Ourselves

Certain practices put us in extended, focused circumstances of shifting away from self and experimenting with simplicity of speech.

These practices allow the Holy Spirit to retrain the heart, the mind, and the body (mouth and gesturing hands) at the same time so that they all work together in harmony. Here are a few practices to consider.

Silence. Extended times of silence retrain our mouths. Being silent in community is especially helpful because it relieves us of the burden of making small talk and quiets our compulsions to impress others through our words. This is an ideal time to journal about how we use speech to try to adjust others' opinions of ourselves.

If you attempt situational silences (not having the last word or not giving your opinion unless asked), you may need to cheat for a while with grins and winks. When we're first learning to simplify our language, these unspoken communications help us do it "as we can, not as we can't."

Pausing. Silence, in the form of a pause, gives us time to consider several issues. The first is timing. Jesus' directive, "Be wise as serpents and innocent as doves" is partly about the snake's wisdom in timing (Matthew 10:16, NRSV). The snake waits for its prey and never chases it down. So I ask God, *Is this the best time to speak up?* We wait for a sense of rightness. If you're unsure, try this suggestion: When in doubt, wait.

Pausing also reminds us to rely on God for what to say, especially in sticky situations. Jesus warned his disciples, "But when they arrest you, do not worry about what to say or how to say it. At that time *you will be given what to say,* for it will not be you speaking, but the Spirit of your Father speaking through you" (Matthew 10:19-20, italics added). We usually don't hear what is "given" to us unless we slow down, pause, and wait on God.

Finally, pausing gives us time to ask God *what* to say, if anything. The first thing that pops into your head may not be wise or loving. When my mother died, I found the lengthy responses of people to be a burden I could not carry. My head was full of details about the situation that I could not share, but people persisted in telling me stories of the deaths of their relatives. I knew these people meant well, but I could not bear all their words in addition to my concerns. Outside of my dear family, only one person seemed to pause and ask God, *What does Jan need?* That friend did not chatter at me but waited for me to talk. When I couldn't, she simply sat with me in silence and then hugged me. That was exactly what I needed: no words, just a powerful Spirit-drenched presence.

Reflection and confession. If we ask God to reveal to us when we use too many words, the Holy Spirit will tell us. Once when I discussed this with my husband, he informed me the next day of an instance I spoke up when I could have been quiet. I wanted to protest that I was innocent, but I was, after all, learning to be quiet. As I prayed about what he said, I thought of even more instances he'd missed in which I should have been quiet! I found myself thanking him for telling me about this.

When God reveals to us our showy speech, our self-interested motives may surface: self-importance, pushiness, disregard for the other person. After confessing these, we can ask God to help us plan the next step. For example, that might be putting my hand over my mouth when I want to interrupt. Or I can lean closer and look more tenderly at the one speaking to me.

Prayer. As you begin each day, ponder whom you'll be speaking to. Consider prayerfully which of those people you might be likely to "run over" with language because you want to convince them of something, because they routinely run over you, or because they love you so much they let you run over them. Ask God to help you love and respect these people.

I hesitate to suggest being accountable to a friend about these practices. So much failure occurs in the beginning that such accountability makes us focus on ourselves more than God and God's leading. Instead it's better to rejoice privately with God in the rewards of simple speech: not being so self-absorbed; seeing into the hearts of others more easily; being able to hear the prompting of the Holy

Spirit because we're less chaotic inside.

Talking less sounds ridiculous in our grab-all-you-can-now culture, but in the kingdom of God, less is more. Fewer words are more powerful because the kingdom of heaven is like a mustard seed, the smallest of all shrubs. It may be insignificant, but don't let that fool you! Someday this shrub—this kingdom—will fill the earth (see Matthew 13:31-32). God works in hiddenness now, but the visible, lavish feast is coming.

EXPERIMENTS IN CONNECTING WITH GOD
(Spiritual Practices to Consider)

To EXPERIENCE God's wordless presence

Listening prayer: Wake up early, before it is light, and sit in the silent darkness. Enjoy these secret moments with God.

Meditation: Read John 8:1-11 and enter into the passage. How do you feel during the silence when Jesus squats and writes in the sand? Do you want him to speak, or do you think his behavior is exactly on target?

Practicing the presence of God: Don't listen to music in the car or as you ride the bus. Just enjoy the silent companionship of God.

Study: Explore the times when God is silent (see 1 Kings 19:12, NRSV; Matthew 15:23; John 19:19) or when silence is recommended (see Psalm 4:4; 46:10; Ecclesiastes 3:7; Isaiah 53:7; Habakkuk 2:20; Zephaniah 1:7).

Study: Note the times Jesus was silent during his trials (see Matthew 26:63; Mark 14:61; Luke 23:9; John 19:9) and note the times he spoke up (see Matthew 27:14; Mark 15:5; John 18:36). Why do you think he chose to be silent at certain times and vocal in others? Did it have anything to do with the person asking the questions? What do you think Jesus was up to?

To BECOME one who offers the holy silence and simple speech of Jesus to others

Associating with the lowly: While serving someone needy, talk less and love more.

Chastity: As you converse, take note of any ways you use others or manipulate conversations to feel special.

Confession: Ask God to reveal to you what motives drive the instances when you speak unnecessarily. Confess these and ask God for a next step.

Fellowship and prayer: Before having lunch with friends or going to a party, ask God to help you bless others.

Guidance: Talk with someone who practices simplicity of speech. Ask how the person is helped by this.

Listening prayer: Ask God, *How are you drawing me to care for others with my words?*

Practicing the presence of God: When someone speaks to you, don't respond with the first thing that comes to mind. Pause and ask God to show you how to respond to that person.

Recollection: Before you go to sleep tonight, consider what you have said today. Did you really mean it? What motives lay behind those words?

Sacrifice: Now and then, don't tell a joke you really want to tell. See how that feels.

Service: Consider some of your present ways of serving. Is there a way to do so with more presence and fewer words?

Simplicity: If you're writing a note to someone, see how few words you can use.

Silence: Spend some time in extended silence. If you are planning to attend a retreat with others, ask the leader if all of you can practice community silence for at least thirty minutes.

Submission: What person needs for you to be quiet and listen deeply to him or her today?

Welcoming strangers: When you meet someone new, don't try to impress the person with who you are. Focus on getting to know him or her.

Worship: Enjoy simple songs such as "Taize" or children's choruses. Pause between and sit with them.

QUESTIONS FOR DISCUSSION AND REFLECTION

1. What two words would you want used to describe your speech (as George Fox was described with "fewness" and "fullness")?
2. Consider the last time you said too much. What was going on in your head? What were your motives?
3. In what situation (or with what person) do you most need to practice simplicity of speech? How do you think it will help that situation (or person)? How will it help you be attentive to God?
4. What does this chapter lead you to want to pray? Be specific.
5. Which of the experiments listed do you see yourself trying out this week?

❧

16   Engaging Artist

What if daffodils were gray, tulips were sepia, and the bright magenta bougainvillea bush outside my window was the color of dishwater? What if Jesus had taught using only explanations and analyses without stories or metaphors (never saying, "I am the light of the world")? What if the Sermon on the Mount was worded like regulations in the Internal Revenue Service tax code? What if instead of healing people, Jesus wrote up a detailed herbal-pharmaceutical index for major diseases?

When the Word "pitched his tent among us," he spoke and acted in ways that were beautiful (John 1:14, literal translation). Jesus talked about such beauty when he announced himself to be the "good shepherd" (John 10:11,14). The word for *good* that John chose means not only intrinsically good but fair or beautiful (*kalos*).[1] This beauty probably did not refer to Jesus' appearance but to the attractiveness of what he did and the compelling power of his love.[2] Jesus enacted the good and the true and the beautiful "life that really is life" (1 Timothy 6:19, NRSV). You and I are invited to participate in this beautiful life.

THE ARTIST-TEACHER

Jesus lived and taught with beauty as a storyteller, poet, screenplay writer, and street-theater actor. Art (which includes stories, poetry, and drama) expresses ideas about which a simple explanation will not do. Jesus' radical message required drama and symbols to be heard and absorbed. We can sympathize with these first-century listeners who expected to hear messages about military revolt but instead were told to love their enemies, turn the other cheek, and go the extra mile. "How do you get across a message as radical as that?" asked N. T. Wright. "In two ways in particular: by *symbols* (particularly *dramatic actions*) and by *stories*. Jesus used both."[3]As a storyteller, poet, screenwriter, and actor, Jesus presented his radical but beautiful message in delightful ways.

Jesus, the Storyteller

The characters in Jesus' stories are riveting. I see myself acting most like the self-absorbed ones: sulking because other supposedly undeserving people have more than I (the older brother in the prodigal son story); whining about people who owe me a little something when others have given me grace and forgiven my debts of discourtesy (the unforgiving servant); and focusing my thoughts endlessly on trying to get the best deal instead of on how I can bless others (the rich fool).

But Jesus' creation of selfless characters is more remarkable because as a playwright once explained to me, inventing good characters is much more difficult than inventing bad ones. Good characters seem unreal because people don't identify with them. But Jesus cloaked his good characters' virtue in selflessness rather than its frequent clothing of self-righteousness. Two of my favorite "people" in the Gospels are ones Jesus made up: the compassionate unself-conscious good Samaritan and the greathearted father in the prodigal son story. Neither was a goody-goody. Both were generous, unassuming givers who never thought about being good; they just were.

Jesus used stories not so much to give information as to cultivate transformation in his listeners. The parables helped people see themselves and the world in a different way. They elicited responses such as this one to the prodigal son drama: *I'm like the older brother. I have God's presence with me all the time, but I don't pay attention. Now that someone else "gets" God, I scoff at him.* The parables charmed listeners into interacting with the drama, and they acted as artful invitations to believe and trust. "Where head-on attack would certainly fail, the parable gain[s] entrance and favour which can then be used to change assumptions which the hearer would otherwise keep hidden away for safety."[4] As hidden assumptions are exposed, people find the desire to change.

Christ, the Poet

In Denise Levertov's poem "What the Fig Tree Said," she takes the role of the fig tree Jesus cursed. She scolds listeners for misunderstanding that she (as the fig tree) was honored to serve Christ who, after all, was a poet who made use of images and metaphors. She reproaches listeners for not having the right juices for bearing fruit as she had not, but also for not understanding Jesus' lyrical way of showing them this truth. Speaking as the fig tree, she brags, "I served Christ the Poet."[5] Reading her poem makes me picture a universe with trees lined up to serve Jesus as a metaphor — did they rejoice to see Jesus and clap their hands (see Isaiah 55:12)? Like this cursed fig tree, many of us lack the right fruit (although we fool people because we have so many green leaves to show off), but this holy Jesus can transform us. We are like the listeners Levertov scolded. We drain out the drama and beauty of who Jesus is by missing his invitation as well as his deeper, resonant way of presenting truth.

To woo us into the kingdom, Jesus chose his symbols (concrete items used to describe spiritual truths) carefully. He portrayed the kingdom of God as a celebration, even a marriage feast (see Matthew 22:2), but an odd sort of feast that drew people from east to west, which included claptrap Gentiles sitting alongside the beloved Hebrew patriarchs (see Matthew 8:11). Only poetry and images will do for a task of communicating "something so qualitatively, dramatically different that it demands a radically different form."[6] Art doesn't beat you on the head with truth. It invites you to taste truth before you know exactly what it is.

Lest anyone be put off by poetic language, Jesus chose familiar symbols and images already rich in meaning to his listeners so they could immediately and intuitively understand what he said. But Jesus put a new twist on accepted ideas. To people whose staple of life was bread, he called himself the Bread of Life. Then they could understand they could not survive without him because he was essential to their ongoing life (see John 6:35,48). To people familiar with the drama of animal sacrifice, he called himself the Lamb of God, which drew them to slowly understand that he intended to sacrifice himself for them (see John 1:29). To farmers who had suffered through poorly producing fields, he described a field "ripe for harvest" that would fascinate and excite them (John 4:35).

In choosing these symbols, Jesus favored the created order: trees (fig and mulberry), seeds (mustard and wheat), vines (grape and fig, both branch and fruit), crops (wheat), sheep, goats, snakes, and birds (sparrows, doves). He pulled in everyday, nature-related vocations (farmer, vineyard-grower, shepherd). With his high esteem for creation, the wildflower lily was more beautiful than the most exquisite spectacle prized in his culture (Solomon in all his splendor; Matthew 6:29). Today he might say that a little field lily he just happened to pass on the road was more beautiful than a sunset in Maui, a supermodel, or a car fresh from the factory. What's more, he would believe it. Such is life in the kingdom of God.

Through metaphors Jesus explained spiritual realities in flesh-and-blood terms to flesh-and-blood people, saying, "I am . . ."

the Door (the entrance into the kingdom of God, into heaven), the Way (the path to take), the Good Shepherd (who surrenders his own self for your well-being); the Light of the World (the only way to see God as God truly is, to see ourselves as we truly are, to see reality as it truly is) (see John 10:9; 14:6; 10:11,14; 8:12).

Such symbols and metaphors speak to the creative, imaginative parts of ourselves that are often closed off to God but open to temptation. They help us grasp what is almost too much to grasp otherwise. More than one symbol helps, as Lewis pointed out: "God is more than a Person [and we tend to] imagine the joy of His presence . . . in terms of our present poor experience of love, [so we need] a dozen changing images, correcting and relieving each other."[7] Just when we've settled on that cozy image of Jesus as the Good Shepherd, we need to consider Jesus as a majestic bronze-footed deity with a voice like rushing waters (see Revelation 1:15). On the one hand, Jesus is a chosen servant who won't break a bruised reed or cause violence in the street; but on the other, he's a burglar and felon who invades a home, ties up the homeowner (the enemy), and steals the plunder (see Matthew 12:18-21,29). Heaven is a place of unimaginable glory but also of refining fire (see 1 Corinthians 3:13-14). Contrasting symbols correct, adjust, complement, balance, and blend with each other so that we are more likely to glimpse the Three in One as "the most pure, the most simple, the most spiritual of all essences" yet "inconceivable in his mode of existence, and indescribable in his essence."[8]

Jesus, the Screenplay Writer

Jesus let events unfold in such a way that they brought delight to the soul, helping people discover reality for themselves. Consider the post-resurrection accounts, especially John's eye-opening moment when he paused at the tomb's entrance and then went inside: "He saw and believed" (20:8). For John, it was a timeless *kairos* moment that would not only live in his mind as an always-vivid picture but also throb in his chest with utmost reality.

Mary Magdalene's subsequent post-resurrection story is full of nonstop drama (see John 20:1-18). Consider it movement by movement as if you are there. After John and Peter leave, she stands crying, but through her tear-filled vision she sees what they did not see: two angels in white, seated where Jesus' body had been placed, one at the head and the other at the foot (John 20:12).

The angels themselves act somewhat offhand instead of doing their typical stately biblical task of announcing important news. Nor do they offer explanations or theological insights. (A few enlightening words about the atonement would have been appropriate.) Nor do they strike a pose appropriate to the occasion by standing with their wings spread out in a majestic way. Clothed in white with an appearance like lightning, they merely *sit* (John 20:12; see also Matthew 28:2). The scene is filled with dramatic understatement, a technique that moves people so much more than overstated embellishment.

These *seated* angels then ask Mary why she is crying (relational interactive drama). As Mary answers them, they perhaps look beyond her, which causes her to turn around and see the gardener. The drama advances as Mary accosts this minor character who might help her with her quest. Unbeknownst to her, of course, he is the missing star of the plot. Jesus has been waiting backstage, so to speak, to assume his role as gardener. This is so typical of Jesus — staying hidden enough to tantalize us to ponder what's *really* going on in the unseen world. He pulls back the curtain just enough to intrigue us and draw us to want to know more.

But the Gardener-Jesus reveals nothing and asks her only the same question about why she is weeping. As Mary's intensity increases to the maximum, she partly accuses, partly demands, and partly takes over: "Sir, if you have carried him away, tell me where you have put him, and I will get him" (John 20:15). She and the women were prevented from helping Joseph of Arimathea and Nicodemus prepare Jesus' body for burial because it would have been improper to mix with them. She was thwarted then, but now she must act!

The delay in finding the body she is looking for makes her speak more passionately each time. Good drama draws out the moment so that each character expresses clearly what he or she wants. Such suspense makes us listeners and readers want to jump onto the stage (or into the page) and tell the characters what they are not telling each other. Have you ever thrust your novel down, run from the television set, or hidden your eyes during a movie, thinking, *I can't take it!* because the suspense is too great?

Yet all is revealed to Mary with one word as her name is spoken in Jesus' familiar Galilean accent. Clarity descends. Imagine the look on Mary's face — delight, rapture. Her response is also one simple word: "Teacher!" She apparently then grasps this body she has been so determined to find. The drama ends with Jesus sending this purposeful, singlehearted woman on the first apostolic mission: "Go tell the guys what they missed by not waiting and seeking as you had the capacity to do." As she leaves, is she even more overwhelmed than she was the day Jesus cast those seven demons out of her (see Luke 8:2)?

Consider that Jesus could have simply held a board meeting where the disciples were staying. Or the angels could have recited the exact order of events, newspaper-style, to Peter and John and Mary. Why did Jesus orchestrate all this drama — the longing, the discovery, the holding of one's breath, the come-to-realize moments, the hidden intrigue, and the whack-on-the-head realization? Because that's how interactive, personal relationships work: drawing, wooing, temporary withdrawals, passionate gestures, and concluding smiles of understanding. Dramatic back-and-forth movements of coming and going compel people to cry out what they do not know is buried within themselves. This was Mary's experience with Jesus, and it is to be ours even now today.

Connecting with God is not about receiving orders from heaven but is packed with back-and-forth personal interaction. The Bible is a divine love story, "a novel in which, though the scene is set, the plot well developed, and the ending planned and in sight, there is still some way to go, and we are invited to become living, participating, intelligent, and decision-making characters within the story as it moves toward its destination."[9]

Jesus, the Actor and Director

Nearly everything Jesus did could be classified as street theater — enacting truth on the stage of everyday life for others to see. As a skillful actor and movie director, Jesus plotted his movements carefully. He created silence as he moved around washing the disciples' feet, allowing them to long for (or dread) his squatting in front of their feet. Like an actor making a cameo appearance, he played the role of the mysterious stranger on the shore who just happened to know where the fish gathered (see John 21:4).

All his actions were laden with messages and meanings. Instead of lecturing people on temple use or how he was really the Lord to which the temple pointed, he cleansed the temple as if it were his own to purify. Instead of telling the disciples he was Lord of the heavens and the earth, he demonstrated it by calming the storm on the Sea of Galilee.

Jesus' triumphal entry into Jerusalem was "an acted narrative of the well-known biblical prophecies."[10] It was "carefully planned and staged so as to make exactly the right point." The animal he chose echoed the prophecy in Zechariah 9:9. "Like the tomb in which Jesus would lie a week later (Luke 23:53), [the donkey] had never been used before."[11] Jesus' prophetic actions told truths without using words so that people responded from within, just as the disciples responded by throwing their cloaks over the donkey (see

Luke 19:30,35-36). His *actions* told the disciples that he was indeed the Messiah, and they believed it.

BEAUTY

Part of the divine lure of Jesus was that of beauty; but such things as beauty, joy, and worship often appear to be a waste of time and money to some, including Judas and the disciples (see Matthew 26:6-13; Mark 14:3-9; John 12:1-8). When the indignant disciples complained of waste in Mary's anointing him, Jesus defended her by saying, "She has done a beautiful thing to me" (Matthew 26:10). The word used for "beautiful" was again *kalos* (as in the "good" shepherd), which describes a thing that is not only good but *lovely*. A thing might be *agathos* (morally good) and yet be hard, stern, austere, and unattractive. "But a thing which is *kalos* is winsome and lovely, with a certain bloom of charm upon it. . . . Love does not only do good things. Love does lovely things."[12] Jesus personified those lovely things.

Jesus carefully hinted at the beauty of our future reality in particular: "When he finally arrives, *blazing in beauty* and all his angels with him, the Son of Man will take his place on his glorious throne" (Matthew 25: 31, MSG, italics added). For just a moment, he gave Peter, James, and John a glimpse of that future beauty. Tired from their hike up to nearly ten thousand feet, the three saw greater heights: Jesus' praying face changed so that it shone like the sun, his clothes appear as dazzling white as the light, as bright as lightning, whiter than anyone in the world could bleach them (see Matthew 17:2; Mark 9:2-3; Luke 9:29). So fastened were the disciples' eyes to this radiant sight that they didn't fall to the ground until they heard the sound of God's voice (see Matthew 17:5-6). Such beauty is possible "in a Trinitarian universe, one where infinite energy of a personal nature is the ultimate reality."[13] The Transfiguration "must be regarded as the highest revelation of the nature of matter recorded in human history."[14]

Why Beauty Is Important

Perhaps this sounds shocking, but churchgoers easily become bored with what they know about Jesus. They can repeat the stories about Jesus and quote his pithy sayings. They want more. They want to be challenged by hearing something they haven't heard before. They have "topped out," so to speak, and so they supposedly graduate to becoming doctrinal sheriffs, spiritual-warfare monitors, or experts in Second-Coming scenarios. In their boredom, they ache for a little drama.

Yet the much-overlooked, God-drenched drama is available in the interactive nature of our relationship with God. The Holy Spirit invites us to further study and meditate on Scripture and so find ourselves drawn to Jesus' intriguing, beautiful person. As we encounter this winsome Jesus in the pages of Scripture, we want union with God more than ever before. Jesus' power to woo us to himself speaks to what is deep within us. C. S. Lewis put it this way: "We do not want merely to *see* beauty. . . . We want something else which can hardly be put into words — to be united with the beauty we see, to pass into it, to receive it in ourselves, to bathe in it, to become part of it."[15] Lewis continues, "At present we are on the outside of the world, the wrong side of the door. . . . We cannot mingle with the splendours we see. But all the leaves of the New Testament are rustling with the rumour that it will not always be so. Some day, God willing, we shall get *in.*"[16] The stories and symbols we've discussed in this chapter are those rustling leaves of the New Testament.

EXPERIMENTS IN CONNECTING WITH GOD
(Spiritual Practices to Consider)

To EXPERIENCE God's beauty and drama

Celebration: Pray the Lord's prayer (see Matthew 6:9-13) in any version you prefer, ending with verse 13 as it appears in *The Message:*

> You're in charge!
> You can do anything you want!
> You're ablaze in beauty!
> Yes. Yes. Yes.

Meditation: Read John 20:1-18 and picture it happening. Write down the feelings you would have had if you had been Mary Magdalene. Jot down anything else about Jesus that comes to you.

Reflection: As you read a certain novel or watch a movie, watch how it follows the Christological path — the main character begins in an elevated status, lowers self, gives up everything, is lifted to the highest place (e.g., *The Color Purple*) — or displays a redemptive theme of pulling people back from their slide into sin and despair (e.g., *Les Misérables*).

Recollection: Recall the most beautiful places you have visited. What words would you use to describe them? What do you think it was like for God to create them that way?

Solitude: Spend at least an hour in a beautiful place — well-tended gardens, the seashore or woods, or a mountain area. Drink in the beauty around you.

Solitude and practicing the presence of God: Take a walk slowly. Notice every color and texture you can find. Put your hand or face against the texture (e.g., tree bark). Stare at the colors and compare them to others.

Study: Pick a favorite parable or two and notice the details Jesus inserted to make it dramatic. Study its background; what images might have resonated with the listeners? What does it make you want to say to Jesus?

To BECOME one who offers the beauty and drama of Jesus to others

Confession: Admit ways you may have disdained storytelling, poetry, drama, or beauty, especially in God's ability to use them to draw you.

Fellowship: Act out your love for someone rather than simply stating it.

Frugality and reflection: Examine your habits of frugality. Are there ways you are needlessly sacrificing such things as celebration and beauty in order to be frugal? How might you blend them?

Meditation: Pick a good character from a parable. Put yourself in that person's place in the story. What does it make you want to say to God?

Meditation: Pretend you are something Jesus used as a metaphor to tell a truth—perhaps a child, grapevine, mustard seed, field lily, dove, or coin. Why were you so useful to Christ, the Poet? How did you serve Christ?

Practicing the presence of God: Plant something beautiful or draw something beautiful or arrange something beautiful. Talk to God as you do this.

Prayer: Thank God for beautiful things or dramatic stories that inspire you.

Prayer: Find a solitary but delightful place. Read Psalm 145 in a celebratory manner. Do it several times until you've convinced the trees and bushes around you that God loves all.

Reflection: Explore the poetry of Emily Dickinson, George Herbert, or Gerard Manley Hopkins. (You might start with Herbert's poem "Love" and act it out. Hint: God is the host/maître d'. Or simply read it aloud dramatically.)

Silence: Think of a truth that is important to you now. Try to write a poem about it, especially about how it is beautiful or important.

Service: Pray that your service in the community (individually or with a group) will in some way serve as street theater to "confess" the gospel through service (see 2 Corinthians 9:13).

Study: Consider the ruling images in our image-based culture (e.g., the pencil-thin female body, the successful executive). What images might Jesus offer instead?

QUESTIONS FOR DISCUSSION AND REFLECTION

1. What stood out most to you in this chapter? Why?
2. How might this view of Jesus as a storyteller and actor make a difference to you?
3. How important is beauty to you? How has it been appropriately or inappropriately important to you?
4. What does this chapter lead you to want to pray?
5. Which of the experiments listed do you see yourself trying out this week?

✿

17   Transcendent Glory

Have you ever longed to experience one of those dramatic Old Testament moments: God speaking to you out of a burning bush? The sun standing still so you can finish the important task in front of you? Hearing a still, small voice after being overwhelmed by earthquake, wind, and fire? Dreaming but seeing heavenly realities (such as angels going to and fro on a ladder from heaven to earth)?

In an effort to be known personally by humans, God creates some spaces on earth where heaven and earth intersect so that the divine presence is more easily apparent on earth. This occurred, for example, in the tabernacle (the "Tent of Meeting") and later the temple (see Psalm 132:13-14). "The sense of overlap between heaven and earth, and the sense of God thereby being present on earth without having to leave heaven, lies at the heart of Jewish and early Christian theology. . . . The place where God's space and our space intersect and interlock is no longer the Temple in Jerusalem. It is Jesus himself."[1]

Jesus granted glimpses of this overlap within himself by doing such things as calming storms, multiplying food, and reversing the ravages of disease. Today if the Holy Spirit dwells in us, we ourselves become a mysteriously overlapping sphere where heaven and earth meet — a temple or dwelling place for the Spirit. You and I become walking temples, Spirit-carriers, letters from Christ, and outposts of the kingdom of God on this planet (see 1 Corinthians 3:16-17; 6:19; 2 Corinthians 6:16; Ephesians 2:21-22).

GLIMPSES OF TRANSCENDENCE

Jesus' life and actions offered continual hints and clues of this reality from another world. Imagine the disciples' wonder and confusion as they got to know Jesus and picked up flashes of his transcendent kingdom. Some of those glimpses occurred in the matter-of-fact way in which Jesus spoke of other-worldly places. When asked about marriage in the afterlife, he made it sound so obvious and simple: "Well, of course there is no marriage in heaven, for we'll be like angels in that respect." He didn't stop to look it up or think about it. He just knew it because he cocreated it (see Mark 12:23-25). When Jesus asked a question about David, he quoted David so casually that it seemed he'd just talked to his friend David over coffee that morning: "So, by the way, David said . . ." (see Matthew 22:42-44). David, as well as Abraham and Isaac and Jacob, was as real to Jesus as my honeysuckle bush is to me. No wonder when the crowds heard him speak they were astounded at his teaching (see Matthew 22:31-33).

The kingdom of God in its totality — the part we see here on earth now and the for-all-time part we don't see — was reality to Jesus. He not only knew about it but continually invited his disciples to step into this reality: "You're tied down to the mundane; I'm in touch with what is beyond your horizons. You live in terms of what you see and touch. I'm living on other terms" (John 8:23-24, MSG).

Now and then Jesus offered more explicit references to this other reality: "My kingdom is from *another place*" (John 18:36, italics added). He spoke about death in ways that would have made one say, "Huh?": "If anyone keeps my word, he will never see death" (John 8:51). *Never see death?* He understood the circumstance of death so well that he could walk up to a dead boy, talk to him, and *be heard* by him (see Luke 7:14-15)! His transcendence welled up from inside him and he acted on it.

All the disciples got a glimpse of it at his arrest. When the crowd of Roman soldiers and temple police said they were seeking Jesus of Nazareth, the force of Jesus' being and words knocked the soldiers off their feet (see John 18:6). But what did we expect? In the Bible this is what people do when they come face-to-face with God (see Psalm 27:2). If the soldiers were helpless in his presence at this declaration — "I am he" — what would have happened if he had chosen to defend himself? It would have been all over for them. Jesus did not skulk in the background but came forward, standing as a lone, unarmed figure as mysterious fall-down power radiated from him. If he had wanted to, he could have walked through this crowd as he did in Nazareth when they tried to throw him off the cliff (see Luke 4:29-30).

Consider what it would be like to experience the force of Jesus' sheer being as this crowd did. Because we put such stock in words over the weight of someone's presence, we underestimate the silent but powerful essence of a person's being. George MacDonald described this in one of his novels as he showed the impact that an unassuming "singular shopgirl" (Mary Marston) had on the daughter of a noblewoman (Hesper Mortimer): "More powerful than all powers is *being. To be* is more powerful than even *to do.* . . . [Hesper] was filled, not with words or advice or ideas that Mary had *spoken* to her, but rather with an overwhelming sense of Mary's person, her *being,* her true self."[2] In the same way, an overwhelming sense of Jesus' person, his being, and his true self must have caused the soldiers' hearts to pump wildly and their breath to escape them, leaving with them the memory of him for years.

During his trial, Jesus talked about that heavenly connection. As the true High Priest, he stood before the false ones (Annas and Caiaphas) and spoke of the glorious future: "But I tell you, From now on you will see the Son of Man seated at the right hand of Power and coming on the clouds of heaven" (Matthew 26:64, NRSV). As a "sign of life from the hidden dimension of God's world,"[3] Jesus was "peace on wheels," ever inviting us to peace (see John 20:19,21,26).

An Extended Glimpse of God

These glimpses of divinity routinely occurred in Jesus' compassionate actions, such as his coming to rescue the disciples on the stormy sea. Put yourself in the place of the disciples struggling with the oars of their boat in turbulent waters in the early morning hours. You do not realize that Jesus sees you from the mountainside where he is praying. (Distance was never a problem. He healed from afar several times. See John 4:46-54; Matthew 8:5-13; Mark 7:24-30.) Jesus does what compassionate people naturally do — he comes to help you.

But in order to get to you (as a disciple), Jesus has to walk on the sea, which from his overlapping sphere of heaven and earth is not a problem. Even as you're tense and frightened by the howling wind and rocking boat, you see his presence gradually appear in the darkness illuminated by the light of the full moon. (It was shortly before Passover.) Because you and your friends are so terrified, he mercifully hollers, "Take courage! It is I. Don't be afraid" (Matthew 14:27). His mere stepping into the boat causes a double miracle: The winds die down and the boat immediately comes to shore (see Mark 6:51; John 6:21). No wonder you and your friends worship him, saying, "Truly you are the Son of God" (Matthew 14:33). No one has to tell you to do this. That is the effect Jesus' actions have on you. If earlier in the day you were disappointed that Jesus evaded attempts at being made king, you now know he rules what no human king could rule (see John 6:15).

John noted that the disciples are "willing to take him into the boat" (6:21). Did John say this because he or they or you are perhaps unwilling for the first moment or two? Is the majesty of God sometimes too much for us and we're not willing to welcome Jesus as close as he would like to come? If we welcome his capacity to be beyond this world but with us, we too might immediately reach the shore where we are heading (see verse 21). But we have to be willing to take Jesus on board.

Partners, Not Puppets

Jesus' transcendence gets overlooked because he never displays it in a glitzy, Hollywood-style way or uses his connections with magnificence as "something to be exploited" (Philippians 2:6, NRSV). Although he is the "master of the created universe and of human history . . . the one in control of all the atoms, particles, quarks, 'strings,' and so forth upon which the physical cosmos depends,"[4] Jesus keeps a low profile. Even as he walks on the Sea of Galilee's waters toward the disciples struggling at the oars, he plans to pass them by except that they cry out in fear. Instead in his compassion he comforts them and then climbs in the boat (see Mark 6:47-52). The next day when the crowds quiz him about how he got to the other side of the lake, he keeps his water-walking miracle a secret (see John 6:22-27), apparently saving it for those who are best equipped (though still shocked) to savor it.

Jesus doesn't overwhelm his followers with too much of his power and transcendence because his goal is to build a relationship with us, not to subdue us into taking orders. This frustrates many people. They want a hotline to God so they can call God about every decision and "take orders." Then the decision will be "right," and so presumably everything will always go "right" for them.

Helping me understand that what appears to be aloofness is actually respect, a friend explained it to me this way: If you give your children a cell phone at the age of two and say, "Call me whenever you need something or have any decision to make," your children will never develop into adult human beings. Instead you guide your children throughout their lives but you don't interfere minute by minute. You give children room to grow and learn, to make mistakes and develop into individual persons.

However, many people would prefer the cell-phone-for-life approach so that they could automatically do the best thing and never have to think or be themselves. If they had been disciples, they might have wanted Jesus to catch every fish for them. But think what you'd miss in this limited mechanical association — an interactive relationship with Jesus. I'd much rather go fishing *with Jesus* and let him show me how to do it than sit there and wait for him to hand me fish. I'd rather have the divine guidance on how to fish and the thrill of being a partner with Jesus in it — and even the joy of telling fish jokes with Jesus — than a satisfaction of being right because I'm an automated, perfect fisherman.

God builds a relationship with us yet stays separate enough to let us keep all our freedom intact. That separateness allows us to *be truly ourselves*, the ones whom God created and loves. It's important for us to retain this autonomy because God wants us to "be partners rather than merely His puppets"[5] (see Philippians 2:12-13; 3:12). We are colaborers with the Lord of the harvest, not merely spectators (see Matthew 9:37). Admittedly, we are small cogs in the wheel of God's purposes, but we are nevertheless cogs — not creatures being rolled over by the wheel. Jesus told his disciples, "I no longer call you servants, because a servant does not know his master's business. Instead, I have called you friends, for everything that I learned from my Father I have made known to you" (John 15:15).

Jesus came to this earth to redeem it — to pull us back from our slide into sin and despair — and as the body of Christ here on earth, we continue his work (see John 14:12; 15:7,16). We partner with God in loving people and meeting their needs, and God gives us the freedom to choose how we will do that. A follower of Jesus is an assistant to the Great Physician, a shepherd boy/girl responding to cues from the Beautiful Shepherd, a purposeful drop in the bucket of Living Water, a happy crumb of the Bread of Life, a dying cell of the stretched-out body of Christ. But a partner, nevertheless.

Being a partner of God doesn't require any role or position. It's about moving through life living in union with God, bearing his image to the world as we bless enemies and go the extra mile. It's about taking risks every day to love people instead of achieving more, about letting go of what makes us feel secure, about noticing that Jesus has gotten out of the boat once again and following him and saying, "So long. Here I go on another adventure." It's really the only way to live — much better than watching sitcoms or playing video games.

Even if you want this relationship, however, this partnering life with God doesn't come naturally. Even the disciples needed some training, and so just before his ascension Jesus trained them in this partnership. He taught them how to detect his presence in subtle ways and watch for him to "giv[e] instructions through the Holy Spirit" (Acts 1:2). They still had Jesus' bodily presence on earth, but he wanted them to get used to partnering with the Trinity as an unseen reality. In his unexpected ethereal post-resurrection appearances, he was

> making them feel that He is never far away. He does not seem to be there. Then He breaks in upon them, always knows what has happened, always takes charge of the situation, until they never know when they may become aware of Him. They must often have turned at the opening of a door expecting to see Him. They stopped midway in a sentence because they remembered that He could not be far away. . . . They feel that He is never absent.[6]

In this way, Jesus taught them that his transforming friendship continued even when they couldn't see him. Jesus invites us into this same transforming soul-friendship and teaches us how to sense him: "I call you friend"; "Come, follow me"; "I am with you always."

RESPONDING TO GLORY

Between Jesus' divine hiddenness and our lack of sensitivity to the overlap of heaven and earth, we often miss Jesus' transcendence today. This happened even as Jesus walked the earth. The hard-hearted cities of Chorazin and Bethsaida saw numerous "deeds of power" but did not respond (Matthew 11:20-24, NRSV). We wonder how they could have done this. Perhaps they were turned off because Jesus spoke hard sayings instead of entertaining messages. Perhaps they wanted to see just a few more "deeds of power."

It's not unusual for believers to want to be tantalized by more experiences. Many would have voted for Jesus to have jumped from the pinnacle of the temple and float down to earth safely. It would draw a crowd and promote "decisions for Christ." Faith and worship with an entertainment focus suits many people well. Speakers who follow the Disney formula (make people laugh and make them cry) make "audiences" happy.

But such ideas as entertainment and audiences are foreign to the way of Jesus. Watching such spectacles as the "temple jump" (perhaps the disciples could have put together follow-up programs) can never substitute for having a relational encounter with the Holy One, as people did with Jesus (and as I hope you have in these chapters).

God didn't create us to be an "audience" but to be *responding participants* and even *performers* in the act of responding to divine glory in worship. Indeed, God is the audience, watching us and enjoying us as we respond to his great love.

The disciples show us the way of worship by taking in Jesus' majesty and spontaneously falling down and worshipping him when he got back in the boat (see Matthew 14:33). The two disciples who walked with him on the road to Emmaus worshipped Jesus after he disappeared from their sight (see Luke 24:52). The man born blind who was healed by Jesus worshipped him when Jesus revealed his identity to him (see John 9:38). *No one made these people do this; they couldn't help themselves.* Someday we'll do the same because seeing the Trinity "face-to-face" will be so magnificent. Sometimes we talk as if every knee will bow and tongue confess at the point of an angelic gun or out of a sense of obligation or to join the rest of the crowd, when in reality it will be that we can do nothing else. Just as both the demon-crazed Legion and the woman newly healed from her bleeding found themselves falling at Jesus' feet, we'll be so glad to be there too (see Luke 8:28; Mark 5:33).

Even Jesus' death on the cross — a cosmic event that darkened the sun, shook the earth, split rocks, split the temple curtain from top to bottom, and wakened dead people — was and is an occasion for worship (see Matthew 27:45-56; Luke 23:44-49). The centurion understood this and praised God (see Luke 23:47). While many ponder the Crucifixion with pity for Jesus and often sentimentalism, Alfred Edersheim emphasized the need for worship instead. He urged reverence more than tears in response to Jesus' conquering death by submitting to the fullest and bearing himself with divine majesty. Jesus moved from "indignity to indignity" in the beatings, bullying, and belittling:

> All through He had borne Himself with Divine
> Majesty. . . . Unrefreshed by food or sleep, after the
> terrible events of that night and morning, while
> His pallid Face bore the blood-marks from the
> crown of thorns, His mangled Body was unable to
> bear the weight of the Cross. No wonder the pity of
> the women of Jerusalem was stirred. But *ours is not
> pity, it is worship at the sight.* For, underlying His
> Human Weakness was the Divine Strength which
> led Him to this voluntary self-surrender.[7]

Jesus lived a radiant life and died a radiant death.

The Psalms give many examples of how to respond to God's greatness. Israel worshipped by singing, dancing, clapping, shouting, and telling God's great deeds. Temple worship involved art (carvings; see 1 Kings 6:21-35; 7:49-50) and drama (in the family reenactment of the Passover story). No style of worship is more holy than another (quiet or loud, meditative or active, ancient or contemporary), as long as we are active participants and not passive spectators. The goal is to *respond* to God.

The practice of celebration also helps us taste God's majesty. I confess that phrases such as "rejoice in the Lord always" sounded too lofty until I read this translation: "*Celebrate* in the Lord always, again I say *celebrate*."[8] Then rejoicing made sense to me: "Now is your time of grief, but I will see you again and you will *celebrate*, and no one will take away your joy"; "And we *celebrate* in the hope of the glory of God" (Philippians 4:4, John 16:22; Romans 5:2, substituting "celebrate" for "rejoice").

We celebrate God's works, God's greatness, and God's power but also how God has helped us: "But I trust in your unfailing love; my heart rejoices [celebrates] in your salvation. I will sing to the LORD, for he has been good to me" (Psalm 13:5-6).

One way to enter into worship is through meditating on passages of Scripture in which people fell at Jesus' feet. Lie on the floor with hands spread wide and enter into the life of the now-healed but formerly bleeding woman who has been freed from her suffering (see Mark 5:33). Or as you lay your petition before God, lie on your face as others did when petitioning Jesus (see Mark 5:22; 7:25; Luke 8:28). Or even as you unload grief, fall on your face (see John 11:32). At first you may feel odd and want to lock the door so no one catches you, but in time you may find that being on your face before the feet of Jesus is a favorite place to be.

EXPERIMENTS IN CONNECTING WITH GOD
(Spiritual Practices to Consider)

To ABSORB Jesus' transcendence

Meditation: Picture the scene of Jesus walking on the sea (see Matthew 14:22-34; Mark 6:45-53; John 6:16-21) and take the role of a disciple. Be honest with yourself about the fear you might have felt. Are you easily spooked? Would you have thought he was a ghost? Would you have been willing to let this barely earthly being in the boat? Once Jesus got in the boat, how might you have worshipped him?

Reflection: What transcendent moments have occurred lately — moments when heaven and earth overlapped — but you perhaps missed them: seeing a person's character change, seeing a newborn baby, receiving a blessing you truly didn't deserve?

Sacrifice: Give away something you need and watch God supply your need.

Worship: Consider songs that highlight the transcendence of Jesus and receive these ideas within you as you sing them.

To BECOME one who offers the transcendence of Jesus to others

Celebration: Sing to God any of the many songs based on Psalm 103: "Bless the Lord, O my soul." Pause and talk to your soul, reminding it why you really do want to bless God (to thank God and praise God). If you don't know such a song, make one up using those words.

Fasting: Fast in some way, focusing on how this helps you experience the reality of the kingdom of God, rely on God, and live for a few moments now and then in the overlapping, interlocking sphere where heaven and earth meet.

Frugality: Consider if you're participating in inappropriate self-display.

Guidance: Who might help you understand how God is inviting you to partner with him?

Practicing the presence of God: One at a time, pick up some objects in your home (a blender, a ring, a plant) and consider that Jesus "is before all things, and in him all things hold together" (Colossians 1:17). What do you make of Jesus' holding together the molecules in that object? What do you wish to say to Jesus in response?

Reflection and confession: Examine yourself for desires to be tantalized by tingly experiences and confess them to God.

Secrecy: Allow something good about you or a good deed you've done to remain hidden from another who might be overwhelmed by you if he or she knew what you'd done. Talk to God about why hiddenness and secrecy are important.

Service: In your normal avenues of service, ask God to show you how to give people space to be themselves.

Study: Consider which passages in Scripture most speak to you about the majesty of Christ.

Worship: In what setting might you suggest practicing Communion (Eucharist) with someone else?

QUESTIONS FOR DISCUSSION AND REFLECTION

1. What stood out the most to you in this chapter? Why?
2. How might this view of Jesus as transcendent Creator — yet humble enough to leave your will intact — make a difference to you?
3. Why do you think some people prefer a mechanical view of God rather than a relational one?
4. When, if ever, have you sensed being a colaborer with God?
5. How do you most need to respond to Jesus' transcendence? Or what does this chapter lead you to want to pray?
6. Which of the experiments listed do you see yourself trying out this week?

Epilogue

"Draw Me, We Will Run After Thee"

God draws us to enter into the life of God himself. We learn to "run after thee" as we move through soul school, learning what it's like to live with Jesus day by day. Such a life of union with God, abiding in Christ, and living in terms of the Spirit transforms us into people who love God and love others.

All of Jesus' characteristics are evidence of the Trinitarian love that we are invited to taste. As a relater-style Savior, Jesus was patient and kind. He took time to relate to people in a personal way, to listen to them deeply, and to welcome them even if others regarded them as strangers. People found him to be authentic—the "real deal."

As a proactive lover, Jesus was never rude, easily irritated, or a record-keeper of people's wrongs. He was so full of compassion that he went the extra mile, even for people who were public enemies. Out of this compassionate nature, he did not manage people with anger and frustration or routinely look at the world with eyes of contempt. He always protected, always trusted, always hoped, and always persevered.

As a purposeful, confident, intentional Savior, he knew what he was about and did everything with single-minded focus. With unfailing courage, he brought justice and truth to a chaotic world.

As a skilled teacher, he made people think and presented truth in intriguing ways so that it was easier to delight in truth instead of evil.

As a selfless, hidden Savior, he did not envy or boast but died to himself and self-advancement. He was not proud or self-seeking but remained hidden in his selfless service and artfully subtle ways. He spoke simply to give people space to think and discover.

As a transcendent Savior, he never failed but showed up no matter what.

My prayer for you is that you have had interactive, face-to-face encounters with God. And in these encounters, I pray you have discovered depth and textures to Jesus that help you hunger and thirst for him in boundless ways, and that you are thrilled that "the real Son of God is at your side. He is beginning to turn you into the same kind of thing as Himself."[1] In such thirst, may you no longer have to make time to connect with Jesus but will eagerly cross activities off your list so you treasure those moments. When reading the Gospels, may you never think, *Oh yeah, I've heard that. Walking on water . . . sure Jesus did that*, but ask yourself what that moment would have been like and how Jesus might be speaking to you today. May knowing Jesus — allowing yourself to be drawn to Jesus — become the most worthwhile and interesting thing you'll ever want to do.

With the writer of the Song of Songs, we say, "Draw me, we will run after thee" (1:4, KJV).

To Use This Book as a Group Bible Study

You may also want to study and discuss this book as "a curriculum for Christlikeness"[1] — to let Jesus lead you into life with him. This book can easily be used in a Bible study format using the following guidelines:

1. Use the questions at the end of each chapter. (Or you may do two or three chapters at a time; for example, chapters 1–3, 4–5, 6–7, 8–9, 10–11, 12–13, 14–15, 16–epilogue.)
2. After answering the first question, have someone read the central passage (listed below) and then ask, "What about Jesus stands out to you in this passage?"
3. Be sure to take adequate time to talk about which experiments (listed at the end of the chapters) you'd like to try this week.

SUGGESTIONS FOR MAKING THE STUDY EVEN MORE MEANINGFUL

1. Ask participants to read the assigned chapter(s) ahead of time.
2. Include in your discussion (either at the beginning or the end) how your experiments from the previous session went. Don't be afraid to talk about what didn't work. The only way to fail is not to attempt an experiment. People will learn a lot from hearing each other's experiences.
3. Between studies, have participants read not only the upcoming chapter(s) but also the central passage each day.

CENTRAL PASSAGES:

- Chapter 1: Soul School: Will I Ever Change? — Abiding in Christ (John 15:1-17)
- Chapter 2: God *with* Us — Jesus looking at and loving the rich young ruler (Mark 10:17-31)
- Chapter 3: Attentive Listener — Jesus listening to the bleeding woman after healing her (Mark 5:24-34)
- Chapter 4: Authenticity: True Goodness and True Realness — Jesus offering genuineness and purity to the woman caught in adultery and to the crowd around her (John 8:1-11)
- Chapter 5: Welcoming the Stranger — Parable of the Good Samaritan (Luke 10:25-37)
- Chapter 6: Compassion That Flows — Jesus moved with compassion to raise the son of the widow of Nain (Luke 7:11-16)
- Chapter 7: Tough but Tender — Jesus healing the man with the withered arm in the presence of the Pharisees (Mark 3:1-6)

- Chapter 8: Speaking the Truth in Love — Jesus' serenity at his arrest (John 18:1-11)
- Chapter 9: Cheerfully Going the Extra Mile — Jesus casting out the demons from Legion and ministering to him (Luke 8:26-39; Mark 5:1-19)
- Chapter 10: Purposeful Intentionality — James and John asking for the chief seats in the kingdom (Matthew 20:20-28)
- Chapter 11: No Fear — Jesus calming the storm (Mark 4:35-41)
- Chapter 12: Exceptional Teacher — Peter walking on water (Matthew 14:23-34)
- Chapter 13: Hidden Servant — Jesus interacting with the two disciples walking to Emmaus (Luke 24:13-35)
- Chapter 14: Dying to Self — Jesus washing the disciples' feet (John 13:1-17)
- Chapter 15: Slow to Speak — Jesus being silent with the Pharisees when they brought the woman caught in adultery (John 8:1-11); or Jesus using few words to heal the child of the royal official (John 4:46-54)
- Chapter 16: Engaging Artist — Jesus appearing to Mary Magdalene after his resurrection (John 20:1-18)
- Chapter 17: Transcendent Glory — Jesus walking on the Sea of Galilee (Matthew 14:22-34; Mark 6:46-53; John 6:16-21)
- Epilogue: "Draw Me, We Will Run After Thee"

Spiritual Disciplines Glossary and Index

The experiments suggested at the end of each chapter are spiritual practices — specific ways of doing the following disciplines (defined very briefly here). For more information on spiritual disciplines, please consult the many books about disciplines or study them for yourself in *Spiritual Disciplines Bible Studies* (InterVarsity).

These disciplines are ways of entering into the life of Jesus. As you practice disciplines, keep in mind that they interrupt our patterns of living a self-referenced life. In these interrupted moments, you connect with God so that God can do a perfecting work in you.

Associating with the lowly: making personal contact on a regular basis with persons who are disadvantaged in some way. When we do this in love, we are drained of arrogance and pride. (See chapter 5.)

Celebration: rejoicing in God — over who God is, in the good things God has done for us. (See chapter 17.)

Chastity: loving people instead of using them. Specifically we don't use them to indulge feelings of specialness. We refrain from inappropriate sexual acts, thoughts, and desires. We find freedom from domination by sex in our thoughts, in how we respond to the culture, and especially in how we view people.

Community: not a discipline in itself but a result of other disciplines such as study, service, fellowship, guidance, confession, welcoming strangers. With our eyes focused on Jesus in these other activities, we find ourselves bound to others "in Christ."

Confession (and self-examination): admitting what we have done wrong as well as examining the motives behind our actions. We don't beat ourselves up but ask God to show us our next step forward. Sometimes that will include confessing our sins to another person (which builds community) and making restitution. Confession is especially helpful in building authenticity. (See chapters 4, 10, and 15.)

Fasting: abstaining from food (including partial fasts of abstaining from meat or sugar or chocolate) or certain activities (such as watching television or participating in other media activities). It teaches us to be richly content with God when we don't get what we want and to rely on God to provide all that we need. It helps with learning to live without anger. (See chapter 14.)

Fellowship: choosing to be with others for the purpose of loving and nurturing them without regard as to whether we receive anything in return. Authentic, loving relationships mirror the love of the Trinity.

Frugality: trimming away what is not needful so we can turn away from consuming things. It involves examination of motives: Why do I think I need this? (See chapters 10 and 14.)

Guidance: recognizing (and perhaps meeting with) certain people who are being used by God to help us. It also occurs in a general way as we become open to how God's guidance may come to us in odd ways: through the words of a child or an article in the newspaper. Spiritual direction is a specific practice of guidance as two people listen to God together.

Meditation: focusing on the Word of God (or the works of God) so we can welcome with meekness the implanted Word. We embrace the ideas, words, phrases, and images of Scripture and nurture them within us so that we absorb the life of God within ourselves. Every chapter of this book except the introduction contains a gospel meditation exercise. (See chapters 2–17; see also *Savoring God's Word.*)

Practicing the presence of God: recognizing God's presence dwelling in you and within others and in the universe and being attentive to God by responding. "Breath prayers" are a specific practice of this. (See also *Enjoying the Presence of God.*)

Prayer, intercessory: bringing requests for others before God, all the while abiding in Christ and asking God for guidance about how and for whom to intercede. It helps to focus on asking for what is best for someone and to pray broadly for this world God so loves. A form of intercessory prayer is "weeping prayer," when we enter into the heart of God and weep over conditions in the world or in someone's life. Using weeping passages from Psalms and the Prophets can help us do this. (See chapter 6.)

Prayer, listening: waiting with God and delighting in God, being quiet with God and resting in God. At the end of meditation on Scripture, it's often done to let the ideas soak in. It may also include bringing questions before God and living in a contemplative way of listening throughout the day. Such prayer trains us in openness to God. It resembles what has been called the discipline of watching in its active waiting and staying alert for a certain period of time. (See also *When the Soul Listens.*)

Recollection: looking back over a period of time to discern motives or behaviors that we need to bring before God or ways we have seen God work.

Reflection: taking an idea and turning it over to see how it runs through our life. It might best be compared to percolating as coffee does in a coffee pot. As a concrete way to reflect, journaling helps us see in print our thoughts, which can create much deeper reflection. (Journaling can also be a form of prayer.) (See chapters 10 and 15.)

Sacrifice: giving away what is necessary so that we may really miss what we give. We "give more than we can spare. . . . If our charities do not at all pinch or hamper us, I should say they are too small."[1]

Secrecy: not letting our good deeds be known in order to learn humility and to have a secret fellowship with God. (See chapter 13.)

Service: "acts of love done to help those in need."[2] As a discipline, service involves making a regular time of service or habit or way of serving that helps us connect with God or teaches us a particular character trait—most often, compassion and humility. (See chapters 5, 9, and 10.)

Simplicity of life: an outcome of practices of simplicity such as frugality (above) and simplicity of speech. (See chapter 15.) Other practices of simplicity are purposefulness and single-heartedness (chapter 10) because they help us focus our time instead of trying to do too many things or doing whatever we're asked to do. We ask God, *What is it I am called to do?* (See chapters 10 and 15.)

Silence: setting aside regular times to be quiet. Usually practiced with solitude, it may involve as little as sitting quietly for ten minutes after lunch or as much as taking a thirty-day retreat. It can be a furnace of transformation as our thoughts shout at us and we respond by quieting them. Situational silences (not having the last word, silencing the mind while others talk, not giving an opinion unless asked, or not interrupting) are practiced in small increments, but they permeate our life. (See chapters 3, 7, 8, 14, and 15.)

Solitude: abstaining from people's company. You become anonymous and try to achieve nothing. Solitude and silence are foundational to all the disciplines. Because it quiets your soul, it is essential if you are to hear God in Scripture. (See chapters 7, 10, and 14; see also *When the Soul Listens*.)

Study: choosing to live in wonder and curiosity and therefore being a perpetual learner—having "ears to hear." A student is anyone who "genuinely and persistently tries to understand and grasp what is true."[3] In study, we examine the order and process of content and methods and take them into our mind not just for facts but for meaning. Before the latter is possible, it may involve memorization and repetition so that the content is available. Regarding Scripture, it means focusing on it with interest and intelligence. As a personal discipline, it has nothing to do with preparing to teach lessons or take tests. (See chapters 12 and 16.)

Submission: giving up power to others. We stop trying to control people and situations. We submit our reputation to God by not promoting self, pushing people, or using guilt to get people to do what we want them to do. (See chapters 3, 13, and 14).

Welcoming strangers: having an invitational attitude toward others who are usually overlooked and helping them find a sense of home with ourselves. We see each person as Christ, especially those who might be considered a stranger (or even strange!) for some reason. We invite them into our life even if only for a moment. Some equate this with hospitality, but hospitality has become limited to having people in one's home. (See chapter 5.)

Worship: responding to God's majesty in specific ways (such as singing or taking Communion) but also living life with a reverence for God and what God is doing today. (See chapter 17.)

Notes

CHAPTER 1: SOUL SCHOOL: WILL I EVER CHANGE?

1. William Barclay, *The Gospel of John, The Daily Study Bible Series*, vol. 2 (Philadelphia: Westminster, 1956), 243.
2. Andrew Murray, *The True Vine* (Chicago: Moody, n.d.), 82.
3. William Barclay, *New Testament Words* (Philadelphia: Westminster, 1964), 38.
4. Seth Wilson, "Life of Christ" (syllabus, Life of Christ: Year 3, Ozark Christian College, 1971), 477, paraphrasing B. F. Westcott, *The Gospel According to St. John* (Grand Rapids: Eerdmans, 1975), 239.
5. Gerhard Kittel, ed., *Theological Dictionary of the New Testament*, vol. 1 (Grand Rapids: Eerdmans, 1976), 711.
6. J. A. Thompson, *The Book of Jeremiah, The New International Commentary on the Old Testament* (Grand Rapids: Eerdmans, 1980), 442.
7. Kenneth Leech, *Soul Friend: The Practice of Christian Spirituality* (San Francisco: Harper & Row, 1977), 49–50; Edward Sellner, "Early Celtic Soul Friendship Part 3," http://www.aislingmagazine.com/aislingmagazine/articles/TAM19/Friendship.html.
8. I understand that God is neither male nor female, but using an impersonal pronoun (its) is a worse error than using male personal pronouns as common gender, as English does. I apologize for this inadequacy. Such is God's grandness that the English language can't manage it.
9. Leslie Weatherhead, *The Transforming Friendship* (Nashville: Abingdon, 1977), 49–50.
10. C. S. Lewis, *The Weight of Glory and Other Addresses* (San Francisco: HarperSanFrancisco, 1976), 29.
11. Mary Jo Leddy, *Radical Gratitude* (Maryknoll, NY: Orbis, 2003), 127-128.
12. Andrew Murray, *The True Vine* (Chicago: Moody, n.d.), 12, 15.
13. Murray, 40.
14. Dallas Willard, *The Divine Conspiracy: Rediscovering Our Hidden Life in God* (San Francisco: HarperSanFrancisco, 1998), 199.
15. Willard, 54.
16. This practice, as well as breath prayers, is described in my book *Enjoying the Presence of God* (Colorado Springs: NavPress, 1996).
17. Brother Lawrence, *The Practice of the Presence of God* (Old Tappan, NJ: Revell, 1958), 35.
18. Names have been changed.
19. C. S. Lewis, *Mere Christianity* (New York: Macmillan, 1970), 64.
20. Willard, 311, 315.

21. Lewis, *Mere Christianity*, 153.
22. Tom Wright, *John for Everyone, Part 2* (Louisville: Westminster, 2004), 60, italics added.
23. Willard, 267.

CHAPTER 2: GOD WITH US

1. C. S. Lewis, *The Screwtape Letters* (New York: Macmillan, 1970), 74.
2. C. S. Lewis, *God in the Dock* (Grand Rapids: Eerdmans, 1970), 160.
3. Clark Pinnock, *Flame of Love: A Theology of the Holy Spirit* (Downers Grove, IL: InterVarsity, 1997), 30, 35, 55, 59.
4. Mark Shaw, *Doing Theology with Huck and Jim* (Downers Grove, IL: InterVarsity, 1993), 62. Quoted in Stephen Seamands, *Ministry in the Image of God* (Downers Grove, IL: InterVarsity, 2006), 35, as quoted in Larry Crabb, "A Trinitarian Understanding of Sin," *Conversations* 3, no. 2 (Fall 2005): 7.
5. Tom Wright, *Mark for Everyone* (Louisville: Westminster, 2004), 191, italics added.
6. I am indebted to Chuck Miller for making this plain to me.

CHAPTER 3: ATTENTIVE LISTENER

1. Dietrich Bonhoeffer, *Life Together* (New York: Harper & Row, 1954), 98.
2. William Barclay, *The Gospel of Matthew: The Daily Study Bible Series*, vol. 1 (Philadelphia: Westminster, 1958), 356.
3. To learn more about the meditative process of *lectio divina* as well as other forms of Scripture meditation, see my *Savoring God's Word* (Colorado Springs: NavPress, 2004).
4. Bonhoeffer, 97, italics added.
5. Janice T. Grana, "Meeting God in Service," in *The Spiritual Formation Bible* (Grand Rapids: Zondervan, 1999), 304–307.
6. For more information, see www.epiphany.org.
7. Tom Wright, *John for Everyone, Part 1* (Louisville: Westminster, 2004), 148.
8. To learn more about contemplative prayer, see my *When the Soul Listens* (Colorado Springs: NavPress, 1999).
9. Bonhoeffer, 98.

CHAPTER 4: AUTHENTICITY: TRUE GOODNESS AND TRUE REALNESS

1. Tom Wright, *John for Everyone, Part 1* (Louisville: Westminster, 2004), 113.
2. Tradition has described Mary Magdalene as a prostitute, but Scripture does not; however, some think she was that unnamed woman in Luke 7:36-50.
3. Donald Hankey, *The Lord of All Good Life* (London: Longmans, Green and Company, 1918), 64–65, as quoted in Elton Trueblood, *The Humor of Christ* (San Francisco: HarperSanFrancisco, 1964), 89.

4. Wright, *John for Everyone, Part 2*, 66, 95.
5. Richard Batey, *Jesus and the Forgotten City* (Grand Rapids: Baker, 1991), 65–82.
6. Four siblings or cousins are named along with unnamed "sisters" (at least two): James, Joseph, Simon, and Judas (see Matthew 13:55). Whether these men and women were siblings or cousins, they apparently lived in such close proximity that Jesus, as the oldest, would have supported all eight of them, supervising the family business.
7. William Barclay, *The Gospel of John: The Daily Study Bible Series*, vol. 2 (Philadelphia: Westminster, 1956), 186–187.
8. Barclay, 250.
9. Dallas Willard, *The Divine Conspiracy: Rediscovering Our Hidden Life in God* (San Francisco: HarperSanFrancisco, 1998), 285.
10. Saint Augustine, *The City of God*, trans. Marcus Dods (New York: The Modern Library, 1950), 14.13, 460.
11. C. S. Lewis, *Mere Christianity* (New York: Macmillan, 1970), 109.
12. John Baillie, *A Diary of Private Prayer* (London: Oxford University Press, 1956), 75. Exact wording: "I pretend to be better than I am."
13. For more about Jesus' lack of self-consciousness, see Alfred Edersheim, *The Life and Times of Jesus the Messiah* (Peabody, MA: Hendrickson, 1993), 556.
14. Walter Brueggemann, *The Prophetic Imagination* (Philadelphia: Fortress, 1978), 44–108.
15. Andrew Murray, *Humility: The Beauty of Holiness* (London: Oliphants, 1961); C. S. Lewis, *Mere Christianity* (New York: Macmillan, 1970), 108ff.

CHAPTER 5: WELCOMING THE STRANGER

1. Dallas Willard, *Renovation of the Heart* (Colorado Springs: NavPress, 2002), 183.
2. William Barclay, *The Gospel of Matthew: The Daily Study Bible Series*, vol. 1 (Philadelphia: Westminster, 1958), 298.
3. Jan Johnson, *Growing Compassionate Kids* (Nashville: Upper Room, 2001), 26.
4. C. S. Lewis, *Letters to Malcolm Chiefly on Prayer* (New York: Harcourt Brace, 1964), 66.
5. Howard Baker, workshop description, "Associating with the Lowly" (Spiritual Formation Forum, May, 2006).

CHAPTER 6: COMPASSION THAT FLOWS

1. Seth Wilson, "Life of Christ" (syllabus, Life of Christ: Year 3, Ozark Christian College, 1971), 310, quoting J. H. Bernard, *A Critical and Exegetical Commentary on John*, vol. 2 (Edinburgh: T & T Clark, 1972).
2. Tom Wright, *John for Everyone, Part 2* (Louisville: Westminster, 2004), 10.
3. This phrase occurs at least seventeen times.
4. Gerard Manley Hopkins, "God's Grandeur" in *The Works of Gerard*

Manley Hopkins (Hertfordshire: The Wordsworth Poetry Library, 1994), 26, italics added.

5. Seth Wilson, "Life of Christ" (syllabus, Life of Christ: The Final Week, Ozark Christian College, 1971), 358.
6. Tom Wright, *Luke for Everyone* (Louisville: Westminster, 2004), 231.
7. Wright, *Luke for Everyone*, 232–233.
8. Kent Ira Groff, "The Gospel According to Luke: Life of Prayer, Life of Compassion" (introduction), in *The Spiritual Formation Bible* (Grand Rapids: Zondervan, 1999), 1347.
9. Franklin Graham with Jeanette Lockerbie, *Bob Pierce: This One Thing I Do* (Waco, TX: Word, 1983), 77. For more about this, see my *Living a Purpose-Full Life* (Colorado Springs: WaterBrook, 1999), chapters 2 and 5.

CHAPTER 7: TOUGH BUT TENDER

1. N. T. Wright, *Jesus and the Victory of God* (Minneapolis: Fortress, 1996), 570–571.
2. John Chapman, *Spiritual Letters* (London: Sheed and Ward, 1935), 25.
3. Dallas Willard, *The Divine Conspiracy: Rediscovering Our Hidden Life in God* (San Francisco: HarperSanFrancisco, 1998), 151.

CHAPTER 8: SPEAKING THE TRUTH IN LOVE

1. Dallas Willard, *The Divine Conspiracy: Rediscovering Our Hidden Life in God* (San Francisco: HarperSanFrancisco, 1998), 221.
2. Seth Wilson, "Life of Christ" (syllabus, Life of Christ: The Final Week, Ozark Christian College, 1971), 488, italics added.
3. Willard, 153.
4. Kent Ira Groff, *The Soul of Tomorrow's Church* (Nashville: Upper Room, 2000), 91.
5. W. E. Vine, Merrill F. Unger, and William White, *Vine's Expository Dictionary of Biblical Words* (Nashville: Thomas Nelson, 1985), s.vv. "judge" (*anakrino, diakrino*), "discern" (*anakrino, diakrino, dokimazo*).
6. Vine, Unger, and White, s.vv. "judge" (*krino*), "condemn" (*katakrino, katadikazo*).
7. Described in Dallas Willard and Jan Johnson, *Renovation of the Heart in Daily Practice* (Colorado Springs: NavPress, 2006), 116–117.
8. This exercise was originally inspired by a sentence in Frederica Mathewes-Green, *The Illumined Heart* (Brewster, MA: Paraclete, 2001), 92.

CHAPTER 9: CHEERFULLY GOING THE EXTRA MILE

1. Ideas and wording adapted from Dallas Willard, *The Divine Conspiracy: Rediscovering Our Hidden Life in God* (San Francisco: HarperSanFrancisco, 1998), 177.
2. Francis of Assisi, as quoted in Veronica Zundel, ed., *The Eerdmans' Book of Famous Prayers* (Grand Rapids: Eerdmans, 1983), 30.

CHAPTER 10: PURPOSEFUL INTENTIONALITY

1. Dallas Willard, *The Divine Conspiracy: Rediscovering Our Hidden Life in God* (San Francisco: HarperSanFrancisco, 1998), 384.
2. N. T. Wright, *Simply Christian* (San Francisco: HarperSanFrancisco, 2006), 186.
3. Tom Wright, *John for Everyone, Part 2* (Louisville: Westminster, 2004), 22.
4. Dallas Willard, *Renovation of the Heart* (Colorado Springs: NavPress, 2002), 199.
5. For help on working through these questions, see *Living a Purpose-Full Life* (Colorado Springs: WaterBrook, 1999).
6. Tom Wright, *Paul for Everyone: The Prison Letters* (Louisville, KY: Westminster, 2004), 132.

CHAPTER 11: NO FEAR

1. N. T. Wright, *Following Jesus* (Grand Rapids: Eerdmans, 1994), 66.
2. Richard Lischer, *The Preacher King* (New York: Oxford University Press, 1995), 171.
3. Alfred Edersheim, *The Life and Times of Jesus the Messiah* (Peabody, MA: Hendrickson, 1993), 862.
4. http://www.mystudios.com/art/bar/rembrandt/rembrandt-sea-galilee.html or Ludwig Münz and Bob Haak, *Rembrandt* (New York: Harry N. Abrams, 1984), 63.
5. William Barclay, *The Gospel of Luke: The Daily Study Bible Series* (Philadelphia: Westminster, 1956), 194.
6. Agnes Sanford, *Sealed Orders* (Plainfield, NJ: Logos International, 1972), 200.
7. Edersheim, 684.
8. Tom Wright, *Luke for Everyone* (Louisville: Westminster, 2004), 176.
9. Barclay, 194.
10. http://www.mystudios.com/art/bar/rembrandt/rembrandt-sea-galilee.html or Ludwig Münz and Bob Haak, *Rembrandt* (New York: Harry N. Abrams, 1984), 63.
11. http://www.oremus.org/hymnal/i/i024.html.

CHAPTER 12: EXCEPTIONAL TEACHER

1. Wolfgang Simson, *Houses That Change the World* (Cumbria, UK: Authentic Lifestyle Publishing, 2003), 217.
2. Dallas Willard, *The Great Omission* (San Francisco: HarperSanFrancisco, 2006), 183, 186. Or see "Jesus the Logician," http://www.dwillard.org/articles/artview.asp?artID=39. A must-read.
3. N. T. Wright, *Jesus and the Victory of God* (Minneapolis: Fortress, 1996), 639.
4. Wright, 175–176.
5. Seth Wilson, "Life of Christ" (syllabus, Life of Christ: Year 3, Ozark Christian College, 1971), 306, 309.

6. Elton Trueblood, *The Humor of Christ* (San Francisco: HarperSanFrancisco, 1964), 49.
7. Trueblood, 46–47.
8. Trueblood. See page 127 for a list of humorous passages in the Synoptic Gospels that we often overlook.
9. William Whiston, trans., *The Works of Flavius Josephus* (Grand Rapids: Associated Publishers and Authors, Inc., n.d.), 640.
10. Wright, 171–172.
11. Neil Cole, *Organic Church* (San Francisco: Jossey-Bass, 2005), 135–136.

CHAPTER 13: HIDDEN SERVANT

1. N. T. Wright, *The Challenge of Jesus* (Downers Grove, IL: InterVarsity, 1999), 160.
2. Wright, 161–162.
3. Wright, 162.
4. Murray Andrew Pura, note on Luke 24:13-35 in *Renovare Spiritual Formation Bible* (San Francisco: HarperSanFrancisco, 2006), 1929–1930.
5. Pura.
6. Pierre Teilhard de Chardin, *The Divine Milieu* (New York: Harper & Brothers, 1960), 111.
7. C. S. Lewis, *Letters to Malcolm Chiefly on Prayer* (New York: Harcourt, Brace, 1964), 75.
8. Philip W. Comfort, ed., *New Commentary on the Whole Bible: New Testament*, n.d. QuickVerse 8, John 2:4, italics added.
9. Dallas Willard, "The Craftiness of Christ: Wisdom of the Hidden God," in Jorge J. E. Gracia, ed., *Mel Gibson's Passion and Philosophy* (Chicago: Open Court, 2004), 175–176.
10. Gerald May, *Addiction and Grace* (San Francisco: Harper & Row, 1988), 94.
11. Dallas Willard, "Spirituality in Ministry," Fuller Theological Seminary class, June 2002.
12. Willard, "The Craftiness of Christ," 175–176, italics added.

CHAPTER 14: DYING TO SELF

1. C. S. Lewis, *Mere Christianity* (New York: Macmillan, 1970), 110.
2. Douglas Steere, ed., *Great Devotional Classics: Selections from the Writings of Evelyn Underhill* (Nashville: Upper Room, 1961), 10, italics added.
3. Gerald May, *Addiction and Grace* (San Francisco: Harper & Row, 1988), 32.
4. Cornelius Plantinga, *Not the Way It's Supposed to Be: A Breviary of Sin* (Grand Rapids: Eerdmans, 1995), 81–83 as quoted in Simon Chan, *Spiritual Theology* (Downers Grove, IL: InterVarsity, 1998), 73.
5. A. W. Tozer, *The Pursuit of God* (Camp Hill, PA: Christian, 1982), 45.
6. Lewis, 109.
7. Dallas Willard, *Life without Lack*, sermon series on cassette tape, Tape 6, *The Sower's Yield*, Chatsworth, CA.

8. Oswald Chambers, *My Utmost for His Highest* (Westwood, NJ: Barbour, 1963), September 30, 202.
9. Tom Wright, *John for Everyone, Part 2* (Louisville: Westminster, 2004), 48. (As bishop of Durham, Wright understands this truth.)
10. Lewis, 114.

CHAPTER 15: SLOW TO SPEAK

1. William Barclay, *The Gospel of Matthew, The Daily Study Bible Series*, vol. 1 (Philadelphia: Westminster, 1958), 157.
2. James Gilchrist Lawson, *Deeper Experiences of Famous Christians* (Anderson, IN: Warner, 1911), 100.
3. William Barclay, *The Gospel of Mark: The Daily Study Bible Series* (Philadelphia: Westminster, 1956), 27.
4. Barclay, *The Gospel of Mark*, 29.
5. William Barclay, *The Gospel of John: The Daily Study Bible Series*, vol. 2 (Philadelphia: Westminster, 1956), 4. Barclay added that "the Armenian translation of the New Testament translates this passage this way: 'He Himself, bowing His head, was writing with His finger on the earth to declare their sins: and they were seeing their several sins on the stones.'"
6. Seth Wilson, "Life of Christ" (syllabus, Life of Christ: Year 3, Ozark Christian College, 1971), 232.

CHAPTER 16: ENGAGING ARTIST

1. W. E. Vine, Merrill F. Unger, and William White, *Vine's Expository Dictionary of Biblical Words* (Nashville: Nelson, 1985), s.v. "kalos."
2. Tom Wright, *John for Everyone, Part 1* (Louisville: Westminster, 2004), 154.
3. N. T. Wright, *Simply Christian* (San Francisco: HarperSanFrancisco, 2006), 111–112.
4. N. T. Wright, *The New Testament and the People of God* (Minneapolis: Fortress, 1992), 40.
5. Denise Levertov, "What the Fig Tree Said," in *Evening Train* (New York: New Directions, 1992), 111.
6. Luci Shaw, "What Good Is a Poem?", *Moody* (December 1984), 10.
7. C. S. Lewis, *The Weight of Glory and Other Addresses* (San Francisco: HarperSanFrancisco, 1976), 35.
8. Adam Clarke, "The Christian Doctrine of God," as quoted in Rev. John McClintock and James Strong, *Cyclopedia of Biblical, Theological and Ecclesiastical Literature*, vol. 3 (Ages Software, Inc., www.ageslibrary.com, 2000), 10–11.
9. Wright, *Simply Christian*, 186.
10. N. T. Wright, *Jesus and the Victory of God* (Minneapolis: Fortress, 1996), 639.
11. Tom Wright, *Luke for Everyone* (Louisville: Westminster, 2004), 229.
12. William Barclay, *The Gospel of Mark: The Daily Study Bible Series* (Philadelphia: Westminster, 1956), 342–343.

13. Dallas Willard, *The Divine Conspiracy: Rediscovering Our Hidden Life in God* (San Francisco: HarperSanFrancisco, 1998), 254.
14. Willard.
15. Lewis, 42.
16. Lewis, 43.

CHAPTER 17: TRANSCENDENT GLORY

1. N. T. Wright, *Simply Christian* (San Francisco: HarperSanFrancisco, 2006), 65, 94.
2. George MacDonald, *A Daughter's Devotion* (originally *Mary Marston* [London: Sampson & Low, 1881]) (Minneapolis: Bethany, 1998), 128.
3. Tom Wright, *John for Everyone, Part 1* (Louisville: Westminster, 2004), 38.
4. Dallas Willard, *The Divine Conspiracy: Rediscovering Our Hidden Life in God* (San Francisco: HarperSanFrancisco, 1998), 336.
5. Agnes Sanford, *Behold Your God* (St. Paul: Macalester Park, 1971), 31.
6. Leslie Weatherhead, *The Transforming Friendship* (Nashville: Abingdon, 1977), 32–33.
7. Alfred Edersheim, *The Life and Times of Jesus the Messiah* (Peabody, MA: Hendrickson, 1993), 878, italics added.
8. Tom Wright usually translates "rejoice" as "celebrate" in his *For Everyone* commentary series, e.g., Tom Wright, *Paul for Everyone: Galatians and Thessalonians* (Louisville: Westminster, 2004), 130; Tom Wright, *Paul for Everyone: The Prison Letters* (Louisville: Westminster, 2004), 128.

EPILOGUE: "DRAW ME, WE WILL RUN AFTER THEE"

1. C. S. Lewis, *Mere Christianity* (New York: Macmillan, 1970), 162.

TO USE THIS BOOK AS A GROUP BIBLE STUDY

1. Dallas Willard, *The Divine Conspiracy: Rediscovering Our Hidden Life in God* (San Francisco: HarperSanFrancisco, 1998), 311, 315.

SPIRITUAL DISCIPLINES GLOSSARY AND INDEX

1. C. S. Lewis, *Mere Christianity* (New York: Macmillan, 1970), 81–82.
2. Dallas Willard, *The Divine Conspiracy: Rediscovering Our Hidden Life in God* (San Francisco: HarperSanFrancisco, 1998), 289.
3. Diogenes Allen, *Spiritual Theology* (Cambridge, MA: Cowley, 1997), 103.

About the Author

JAN JOHNSON is the author of seventeen books and more than a thousand magazine articles and Bible studies. Also a speaker, teacher, and spiritual director, she lives with her husband in Simi Valley, California (www.janjohnson.org). She holds a D. Min. in Ignatian spirituality and spiritual direction and writes primarily about spiritual formation topics.